PICTURE CREDITS

Photographs on pp. 9, 14, 20, 32, 39, 51, 61, 82 , 95 by Phil Carswell. The images by David McDiarmid are reproduced by kind permission of the Estate of David McDiarmid.

Dennis Altman took the photo on p 38; Alison Thorne, p 88; Henry von Doussa p 96, 97; Marcus O'Donnell p 94. All other photographs by Geoff Allshorn.

ALWAYS REMEMBER

40 years - 40 objects and images from the
AIDS epidemic, 1981 ~ 2021

GEOFF ALLSHORN

With contributions from Dennis Altman, Phil Carswell, Henry von Doussa,
Alison Thorne, Marcus O'Donnell, Paul Cholewinski

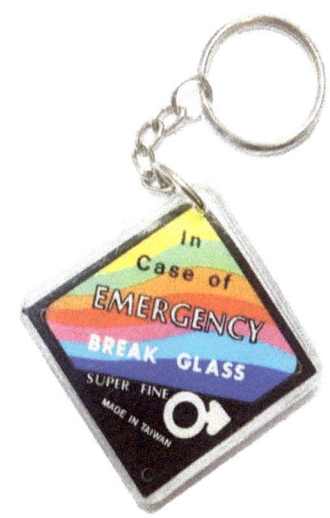

Clouds of Magellan Press | Melbourne

Clouds of Magellan Press, Melbourne. www.cloudsofmagellanpress.net

ISBN: 978-0-6453531-4-3 (paperback)

ISBN: 978-0-6453531-5-0 (eBook)

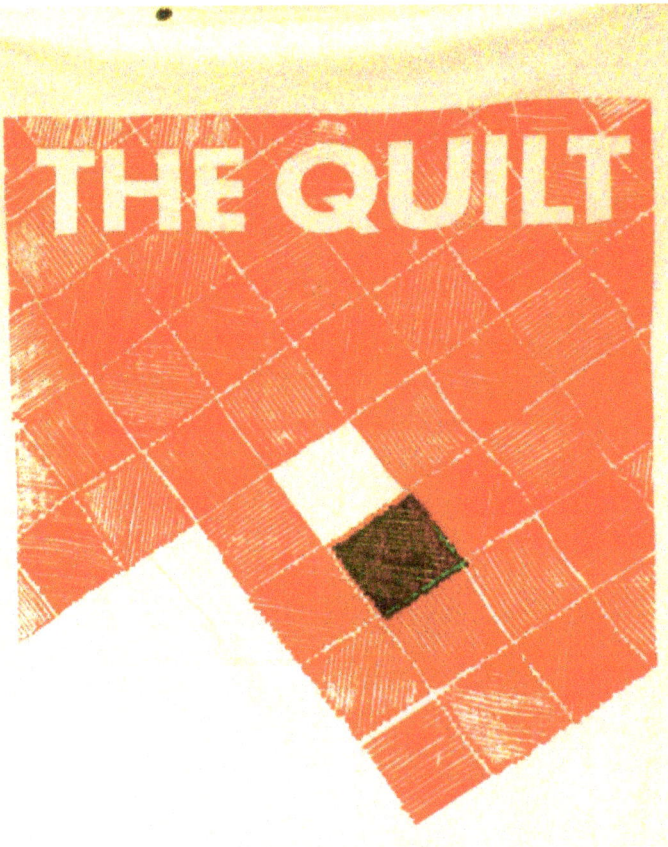

Quilt banner. Geoff Allshorn

PRELUDE

I open the door – the space is now a conference room where once it had been a chapel … I last saw my old friend Alan on display in his coffin in a small side room that now serves as a discussion room…

Entering the main area, I walk to a window curtain and pull it back. There is one small plaque that evidently has not been removed along with all the others that used to decorate this wall, along with all the others once found on nearby external seating. Where have these other plaques gone? Where are these remembrances of past times and past lives? Nobody knows.

I replace the curtain to hide this solitary plaque, like a scientist in the wild replacing a precious endangered animal in its last piece of habitat. I stand in silence and ponder the metaphoric ghosts that fill my mind …

I wonder how many others who were with me that day, celebrating the relaunch of an AIDS garden on the premises, recall that this particular building was once a chapel, paid for by public donations in order to enable those who died with AIDS to have a funeral when their local family churches refused to conduct the rite?

Forty years ago, a worldwide epidemic was unknowingly announced in a newspaper. Unlike COVID-19, this other virus had been unforeseen and undiscovered and was, ultimately, politically stigmatised until it was on track to cause irreparable loss of life. A generation later, it still has no vaccine – although it has treatment options that have transformed the virus into a manageable lifelong condition.

Despite my attempts in recent years to undertake an extensive research project and compile a definitive and all-encompassing history of HIV/AIDS in Australia (or even in Melbourne), the task has proved to be elusive and overwhelming. How does one adequately document the lives and deaths of thousands of people, their tragedies and triumphs, their history and heroism, their pride in the face of prejudice?

Instead, to commemorate the fortieth anniversary of AIDS, I present a series of personal memories and researched writings which hopefully demonstrate that the personal is political. One of the first AIDS books to appear in Australia – *And the Band Played On* by US author Randy Shilts – described the arrival of AIDS as a demarcation point in history that would forever divide those living 'before' and 'after' our world was transformed by a virus.

These are some of my stories and memories, and a few articles I have written over recent years in tribute. Others will have different but equally poignant recollections of how their lives and world were changed. I'd like to thank Dennis Altman, Phil Carswell, Alison Thorne, Henry von Doussa, Marcus O'Donnell, and Paul Cholewinski for helping to flesh out this project so that we could achieve forty images and objects for the forty years since 1981. I would also like to thank Gordon Thompson (Publisher at Clouds of Magellan Press) for his tireless work. Special thanks must go to all my friends, mentors and heroes within these pages, and all the other voices they represent.

This work was supported by an Australian Government Research Training Program Scholarship. Some names in these articles have been changed.

Geoff Allshorn, 1 December 2021

THE FAMILY NEWSPAPER THAT CARES

The Sunday Telegraph

TOPS FOR SPORT

Price 70¢ * (airfreight extra)   SUNDAY, NOVEMBER 18, 1984   Registered by Australia Post — Publication No. NBP0030

EXCLUSIVE — 10 MORE SUSPECTED DEATHS

AIDS SWEEPS THE NATION

NEW FIGURES

Spread of the plague of the 80s

NSW
Confirmed: 22
Suspected: 61
Deaths: 4

Victoria
Confirmed: 6
Deaths: 4

Queensland
Confirmed: 3
Suspected: 10
Deaths: 4

West Australia
Confirmed: 6
Suspected: 1

No reports in Tasmania, Northern Territory and South Australia

THE AIDS crisis deepened throughout Australia yesterday as the search for contaminated donor blood continued and fears rose that the problem is far more widespread than previously believed.

Concerned medical authorities warned that the deadly disease suspected of killing three babies and at least seven men is now suspected of killing even more people.

Their grim predictions headed a growing list of dramatic developments which threaten to engulf the crisis meeting of health ministers and authorities in Melbourne today.

In the latest developments:
● Ten more suspected AIDS-related deaths were announced by the Queensland Health Minister, Mr Brian Austin, following the baby deaths.
● Contaminated blood from the same batch given to the babies may have been sent to Sydney.
● The Premier, Mr Wran, announced he would consider recalling Parliament to pass tough new laws — and even change the Anti-Discrimination Act — to crack down on homosexuals and drug addicts who donate blood.

● Dr Julian Gold, a leading researcher, described the AIDS outbreak as the first major, total epidemic in Australia for more than 50 years.
● Professor Ronald Penny, another leading researcher, warned that the number of AIDS victims was certain to double over the next six months, then double again over the following six months.

● A Gay Army spokesman warned that up to 50,000 Sydney homosexuals could become AIDS victims, based on a Sydney study which showed that up to half of homosexual males could be carriers.

Mr Wran told The Sunday Telegraph that he would also consider banning male donors, and boosting facilities to enable more women to become donors.

Mr Wran said he was not worried about infringing "gay rights".

● CONTINUED P.2

Report by GEOFF McCAMEY, GRANT VANDENBERG, WARREN OWENS and JUDY JACKSON

● **Gay leader: 50,000 infected**

● **Wran: I'll recall Parliament**

● **Expert: Cases will double**

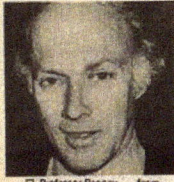

□ Professor Penney . . . fears

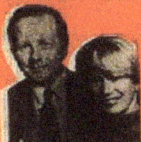

SANGSTERS: The couple with the Melbourne Cup jinx

● SEE PAGES 14 AND 15

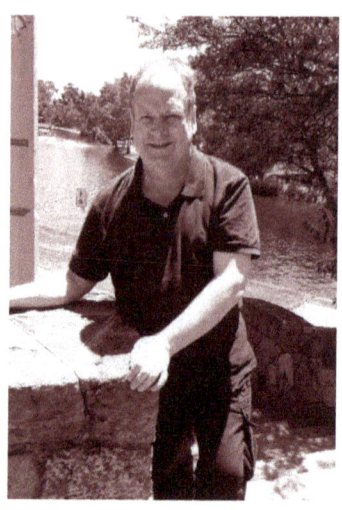

Memorial to Dr George Duncan, River Torrens, SA 2015. Geoff Allshorn

BEFORE

It is a sunny day in Adelaide, and the Torrens River sparkles quietly while individuals and small groups meander casually along the manicured pathways and lawns that line its banks.

There is a casual festival atmosphere in the vicinity. Weekends here seem carefree and friendly. Nobody seems to realise the significance and undertone of violence that is represented by a stone plinth in a raised area on the riverside.

The George Duncan memorial stands as a silent sentinel to past times and past crimes that were undertaken with impunity due to homophobic laws and institutions. I wonder if I am the only person today to pause and reflect at this memorial, understanding the symbolic significance of the triangular plaque in the shape of the pink triangle used by the Nazis to identify their homosexual victims.

The murder of law lecturer George Duncan spearheaded legislative change in South Australia under the leadership of Premier Don Dunstan. It ultimately paved the way for homosexual law reform across Australia – coincidentally at

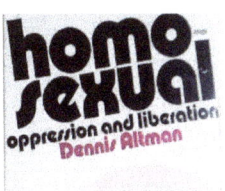
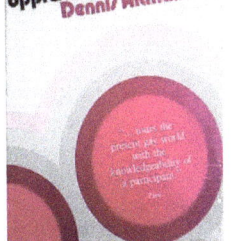

around the same time that a certain virus was making its way, unseen, into Australia.

One significant push-back against traditional homophobia came in the form of gay liberation, sparked in part by Australian activist Dennis Altman and his definitive 1971 book, *Homosexual Oppression and Liberation*. Coming on the back of the UK Wolfenden Report of 1957, and civil rights activism in Australia from Humanists as far as 1966, gay liberation empowered many LGBT people to come out and demand civil rights.

History records the tragedy that their collective mobilisation and sexual liberation coincided with the arrival of a virus that created, for gay men and many others from varied cohorts, the most devastating epidemic (before COVID) in living memory.

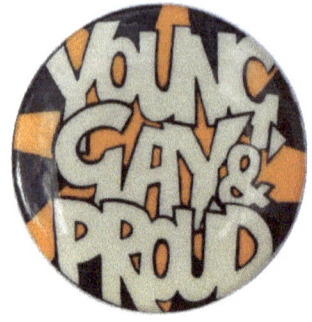

The activist strength that was forged during the gay lib era would be put to its most challenging test in a fiery crucible of epidemic.

Homophobic violence, similar to that endured by George Duncan, was not uncommon across Australia before and after the arrival of AIDS. Possibly the most famous ongoing cases of anti-gay violence took place at Bondi and other locales in Sydney, and many of these crimes remain unsolved even today. Some of those Bondi crimes, and others around Australia, may have been encouraged by AIDS phobia during the epidemic years.

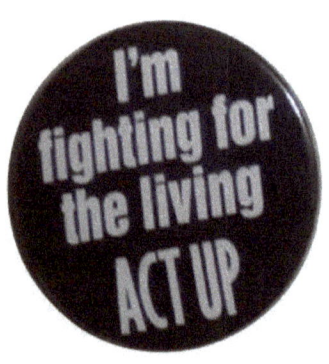

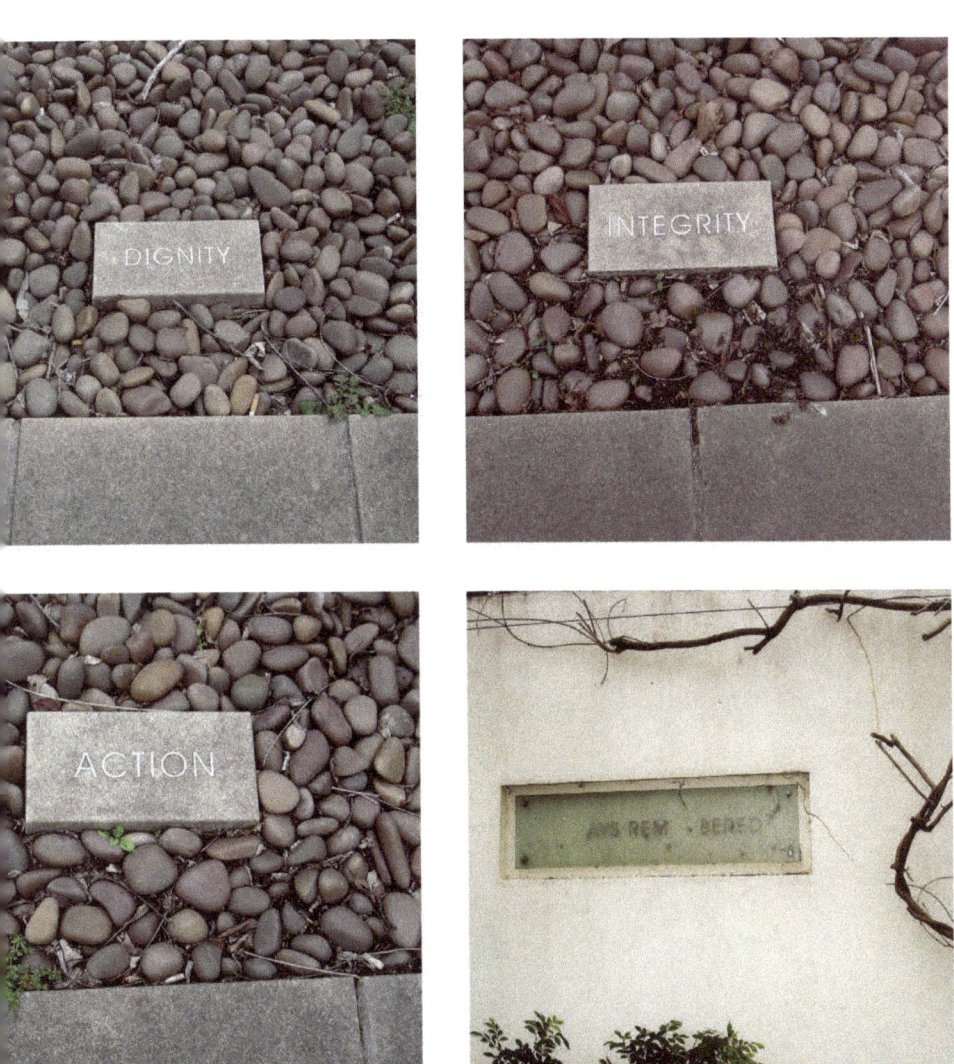

AIDS Memorial Garden, Alfred Hospital, Melbourne. Geoff Allshorn

TOUCHED BY
A PERSON LIVING
WITH AIDS

FIGHT BACK
ACT UP
FIGHT AIDS

SOMETHING HAS HAPPENED

The era of AIDS is recalled often as a time of double epidemic – one of stigma as well as disease. I am reminded of stories about young gay men who were forced by their sexuality to leave home and seek life in Sydney or Melbourne or San Francisco or New York (or some other metropolis) only to have to return home with double whammy news: 'Mum, Dad, I need to tell you something. 1. I am gay and 2. I have AIDS.'

Or the triple whammy 'And 3. I am dying.'

What leaves me breathless is the reported response attributed to a few parents at that time: 'We are more upset that you are gay than the fact that you are dying.'

I told this story to a few younger adults recently and their response was puzzlement: 'I can understand being upset about someone being sick, but why was there a problem with someone being gay?'

We live in clearly different cultural times in Australia these days (ask a LGBT person elsewhere if times have really changed) but I worry that our communal stories are being forgotten in our desire to leave behind the painful days of AIDS.

His name is not recorded in Australia's history books. He was just an average Australian bloke, but he became possibly the first casualty – the proverbial Unknown Soldier – in one of Australia's most frightening wars.

He was born in Australia in 1909, when our nation had barely reached Federation. He spent his infancy during harsh drought, in an era of horse and cart, electric trams and the telegraph. As a young boy, he would have seen older lads – possibly his father and older brothers – go off to the Great War. Later, he would have witnessed those who survived the war returning home to live with possible shell shock or disfigurement – and to face the worldwide pandemic wrongly named Spanish Influenza (not the first or last time that a disease or epidemic would be attributed to a geographic, national or cohort origin).

As a young adult, he saw the opening of Sydney Harbour Bridge, survived the polio era, lived through the Great Depression, and he may have served in World War Two. As an older adult, he saw many changes and challenges: television and antibiotics, automobiles and aircraft. He witnessed the Korean and Vietnam Wars, the Berlin Wall and Cuban Missile Crisis, the Apollo Moon landings, US assassinations and civil rights demonstrations.

His world was shaped by the Cold War and his lifestyle may have been oppressed by McCarthyism. He lived through the early days of Gay Liberation and he may have marched in the original street protest which led to the annual Sydney Gay and Lesbian Mardi Gras.

According to sparse newspaper reports published over a decade later (Davies 1993, Carter 1994), he began to get sick around February 1981. This was around the same time that millions of Australians were becoming distracted by the engagement of Prince Charles to Lady Diana. By the time of the Royal wedding in July, our friend's prolonged illness had developed into a persistent cough and he had pronounced difficulty with breathing.

The illness which struck him was testimony to the international travel that had become a ubiquitous aspect of our modern jet-setting lifestyle, despite the fact that he had personally never travelled overseas. He was afflicted with what was then called *Pneumocystis Carinii Pneumonia* (or PCP, now known as *Pneumocystis jiroveci* pneumonia), a fungal affliction that had first been identified in 1909 – ironically the year of his own birth. It was only after World War Two that PCP began to appear in malnourished children who lived in overcrowded orphanages of post-War Europe – and a link was established between and humans whose immune systems had been damaged or compromised (Shilts, 1987, 34). A symbolic link had also been established between PCP and the concept of war or deprivation – a metaphor which would not be forgotten in the coming years, including in Australia.

All this background probably meant little to our friend, who battled his chronic breathing problem without being aware that others around the world had also recently puzzled their doctors with similar or related medical difficulties. There were many such unknown soldiers in this unknown war, including families, a female Danish surgeon, babies, gay men; people from Norway and Belgium and Denmark and Portugal and France. Although white gay men got most of the media attention, they were merely the tip of a metaphoric iceberg of infection and stigma: the late 1970s also saw a rise of what was colloquially called 'junkie pneumonia' in New York (Maurer, 1992, 1); while early stories included women, sex workers, injecting drug abusers, low income ethnic minority women, African Americans and Hispanics.

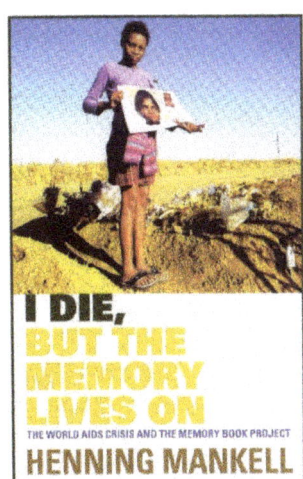

In Africa, the danger had already been spreading silently for years. Preserved blood samples indicate the presence of HIV antibodies collected from varied African subjects from 1959 onwards. Swedish author Henning Mankell reports anecdotal evidence that mysterious ailments were being noticed among men and women in Uganda as far back as the 1970s. The syndrome became popularly known in Africa as 'Slim' due to its associated effects of diarrhoea and weight loss. According to one story documented by Mankell, a young man named Lukas had become afflicted in 1974 with an increasingly-debilitating mystery illness which included swollen glands, weight loss and an outbreak of sores. Lukas, and his two wives, all got sick and died – followed, in subsequent years, by other people in Kampala. One of Lukas' workmates had explained this mystery to his child through a simple but hauntingly significant truth: 'Something has happened' (Mankell, 2004, 52 & 53).

Something was indeed happening – and a killer virus was silently spreading; its first likely identified victim in the USA being an African-American teenage boy who was retrospectively diagnosed some decades after his death in 1969 (Garry et al, 1988), at around the time that the rest of the world was experiencing the scientific and social watersheds of Apollo 11 and the Stonewall riots.

Our anonymous Aussie battler would most likely have been totally oblivious to this community of suffering when he was admitted to a Sydney hospital in August 1981, after six months of deterioration. He died the following month, aged 72. A new pandemic had arrived in Australia and silently claimed its first casualty.

Twelve years later, doctors tested a preserved medical specimen that had been collected from the patient in January 1980. Using a test which had been unavailable and unimaginable back in 1980, they discovered that the patient had died of a condition which we now call AIDS. Yet when this patient died, AIDS had barely even been recognised as a problem overseas; it was still so new and mysterious that it had not yet been accurately identified, nor even have a name (Willis 2020); and its existence in Australia had been unknown at that time. This led Australian doctors to make a worrying declaration in 1994 following their retrospective diagnosis of this patient:

Whether this represents an isolated case in a man who progressed rapidly because of his relatively advanced age, or whether HIV was present earlier in Australia than previously thought, remains unanswered. (Gerrard et. al., 1994)

'Patient X' had never had a blood transfusion nor any record of injecting drug use – and yet his blood told a chilling story. Somehow, he had been exposed to the virus here in Australia in late 1979 or possibly earlier (Carter, 1994; Davies, 1993). His actual biographical details are speculative, including whether or not he may have been gay, because – not unlike many LGBT people living in those homophobic times – little is actually known about him:

There is not a lot of detail about his life in case notes, no mention of next of kin or any hospital visitors. We don't even know his real name. (Willis, 2020)

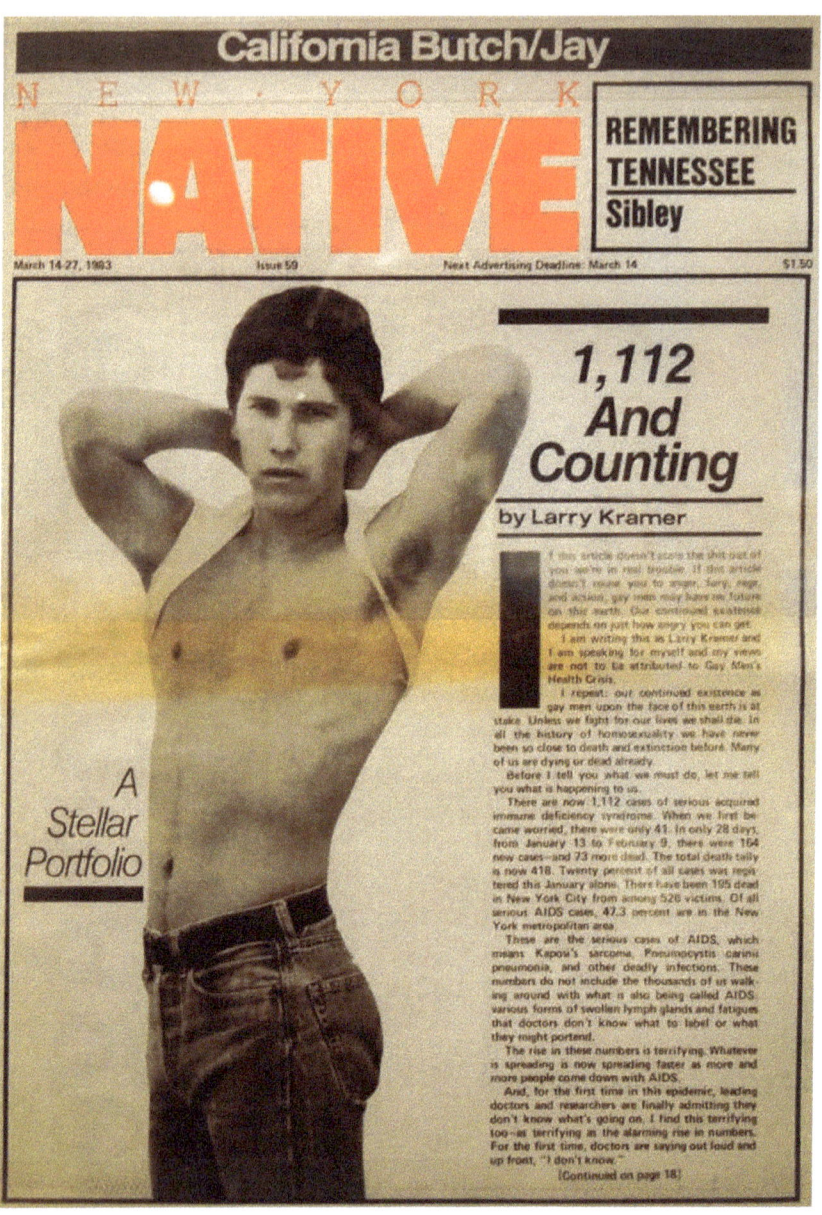

Front page of NY NATIVE, March 1983, with Larry Kramer's call to action – 'If this article doesn't scare the shit out of you we're in real trouble ...'

DEMARCATION

On 3 July 1981, the emerging catastrophe was announced to the world. *The New York Times* – not the first to publish an article, but the first to publish one that gained widespread public attention – announced that a 'rare cancer' had been found in 41 homosexuals (Altman, 1981). It revealed the worrying aspects of an emerging pattern: rare diseases were being caught as an indication of a compromised immune system among young gay men who should not normally be victims to such medical oddities (McKie, 1986, 21 & 22).

On that very same day, on the other side of the world, Sydney's gay publication, *Sydney Star,* also published a much smaller news item, entitled, 'New pneumonia linked to gay lifestyle' (Author unknown, 1981). History would reveal a tragic irony in the fact that this latter article appeared beneath an advertisement featuring a gay man with an 'R.I.P.' tattoo on his arm. These were Australia's last days of innocence before the arrival of an epidemic that would invoke a great mortality, fear and stigma. Soon, stories and rumours began to circulate regarding strange illnesses among gay men in Melbourne and Sydney hospitals (Allshorn, 2011, 4 & 5).

One of the Australians who read the *New York Times* that day was John Foster, a Melbourne historian who was on study leave in New York City. He later recalled the day which would forever announce the public arrival of slow-creeping catastrophe into the lives of millions of people around the world:

> *Doctors in California and New York had diagnosed among homosexual men forty-one cases of a rare and often rapidly fatal form of cancer. The cancer appeared in violet-coloured spots which might be taken for bruises and which often turned brown before they spread throughout the body … This was definitely not serious. Or at least,*

it did not concern me. I was not in the violet-spot league. (Foster, 1993, 39 & 40).

Three weeks later, on 25 July 1981 (ibid, 41), John Foster was to meet young Juan Cèspedes, and this meeting would change both their lives. They struck up a casual friendship which quickly became a long-term relationship. Since his arrival in New York as a refugee some twelve years earlier, Juan had subsequently been unable to realise his personal ambition of becoming a dancer due to the prejudice of others and following an accident with a New York taxi cab. His relationship with the Australian academic John Foster would provide him with new hopes – and it would provide John Foster with companionship and confidence.

Foster's mistaken belief that he and Juan were not in any danger of belonging to the 'violet-spot league' (Kaposi's sarcoma, an AIDS-related opportunistic infection) was a continuation of the same confidence which had been experienced by a younger Juan Cèspedes in the days of Gay Lib – and yet they were later to discover that such confidence and dreams would ultimately turn into ashes. Their fate would be shared with thousands of other Australians, and millions of people around the planet.

In 1981, a new epidemic had crept silently into our world, creating a concurrent epidemic of discrimination, stigma and disempowerment, and giving rise to community activism that has never been matched before or since. Ebola, SARS and COVID are not the first epidemics in living memory, but our response to these others has been shaped – rightly or wrongly – by the lessons we have learnt (or failed to learn) from HIV/AIDS.

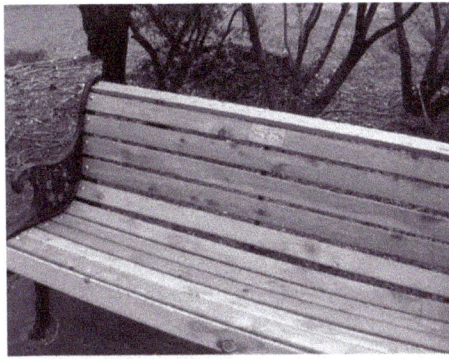

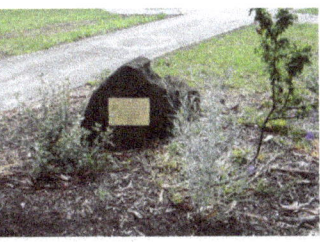

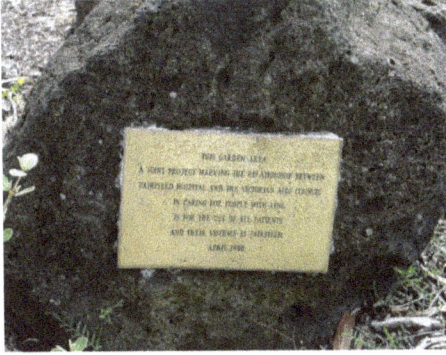

AIDS Memorial Garden, Fairfield, 2010. Former Fairfield Hospital site. Geoff Allshorn

TV OR NOT TV

In recent times, friends in the science fiction community have complained in social media that some cohorts of audiences are being victimised and excluded from popular entertainment. Doctor Who *has recently been a woman.* Star Trek *features women of colour and a gay couple. In* Star Wars, *an embittered Luke Skywalker has been replaced by young and idealistic Rey. 'Where are we?' cry affluent, entitled, straight white males from the audience fan base, 'Why have we been excluded?'*

Welcome to my world, I reply. Now you know what it has been like to be anything other than a straight white male on television since forever. Indeed, why have my HIV+ friends been almost completely excluded from Australian TV to this day?

Early representations of AIDS on Australian television initially tapped into our national rural mythology. AIDS arrived fleetingly in the fictitious Australian outback town of

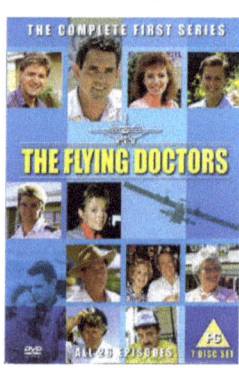

Cooper's Crossing in the television series, *The Flying Doctors*, then it visited the equally fictitious rural town of Wandin Valley in *A Country Practice*. Both stories contextualised AIDS as a remote threat affecting the metaphorical 'other' instead of acknowledging HIV as a real-life, predominantly urban and very human problem. In *The Flying Doctors* (1986), a gay male guest character arrives in town and discloses that he has AIDS and is returning home to die before the end of the episode. He and his partner are social outcasts who lack the supportive AIDS networks that were actually emerging in urban gay communities. Two years later, the same writer created a story for *A Country Practice* in which a major character had an adult HIV-positive daughter, who visited her father before dying from a drug overdose. This second story may have resulted from a desire to promote the concept that AIDS is more than just a 'gay disease', in line with the 'Grim Reaper' campaign which warned that AIDS had the potential to spread beyond marginalised groupings. However, the story theme in *A Country Practice* may also provide evidence of some reluctance on the part of the series producer to portray 'a homosexual AIDS victim [as] a 'goody' and sympathetic'.

A Country Practice echoes American television's treatment of the same issue. Up until 1988, the only characters to die of AIDS in US daytime soap operas were women. This avoidance of homosexuality through a disproportionate portrayal of women paralleled a concurrent trend in Australia's cultural response to AIDS. Shortly after the Grim Reaper campaign, a young heterosexual woman named Suzi Lovegrove was shown living (and 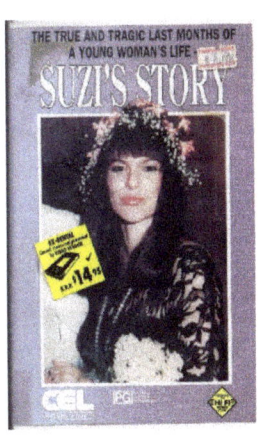 dying) with AIDS in the documentary *Suzi's Story*, while Australia's most prominent spokesperson on AIDS at the time was media celebrity Ita Buttrose. One of Australia's biggest AIDS scandals featured Eve Van Grafhorst, a young girl with HIV who was banned from her kindergarten. This over-representation of women reflect the Australian social tradition of female gender roles which allow for the public expression of 'softer', more compassionate representations of socially stigmatized sexualities and diseases. It also denied the existence of the majority of people who were living with AIDS.

The Australian Broadcasting Corporation later commenced a long-running soap opera called *GP*, which was set in the 'urban milieu' of modern Sydney. One episode, *Toss A Coin*, featured a story about a five-year-old girl who had contracted paediatric AIDS and faced prejudice and discrimination at her school. This story may have been a response to the real-life case of kindergarten girl Eve Van Grafhorst, and the episode won the 1989 Human Rights Award for TV Drama. Another episode, *Mates*, featured a gay

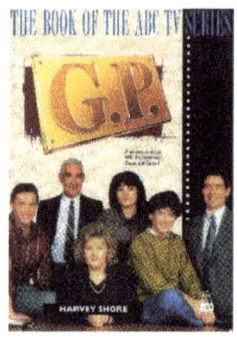

male couple coming to terms with an HIV diagnosis for one of the partners. Their storyline concluded in the episode *Lovers*, which presented the reality that Australian law did not recognise gay partners, and that estranged heterosexual family members had overriding legal rights as next of kin. *Lovers* reportedly won a number of awards including the 1990 'Penguin' Award for Best Direction. The topic of that episode – same sex relationships – became a real-life issue for many LGBT couples during this era, leading to the movement that eventually achieved marriage equality.

Other Australian television forays into HIV/AIDS include *E Street* (Channel 10, 1991), *Home and Away* (Channel 7, 1996), *Breakers* (Channel 10, 1997), *Pacific Drive* (Channel Nine, 1990s), *Stingers* (Channel 9, 2000) and *Packed to the Rafters* (Channel 7, 2009); all of which featured storylines about heterosexual women being threatened or affected by HIV. Conversely, Channel Nine's *Chances* soap opera ended ignominiously in 1993 when the final episode revealed that its resident villain 'was responsible for unleashing AIDS'; and *Blue Heelers* (Channel 7, 1995) featured a heterosexual man being threatened by HIV. Australian television has resisted including a major and continuing HIV-positive character (let alone a gay man) in any prominent Australian fictional TV series, a notable omission when one considers that overseas, the South African version of the children's series *Sesame Street* has included an HIV-positive muppet.

Given that Australian television featured a gay character in *Number 96* a decade before the arrival of HIV/AIDS ('Don Finlayson' played by Joe Hasham), one wonders why locally produced television appeared to go backwards in its portrayal of difference during the era of AIDS.

A tragic test of friendship

By DAN McDONNELL

THE most tragic way to find out who your friends are is to suffer from AIDS.

The head of one of Sydney's biggest AIDS units told at the weekend of how the so-called friends of one patient deserted him when he most needed them.

Prof John Dwyer said the man died "of a broken heart" 48 hours after his friends discovered inadvertently that he had AIDS.

The man, a prominent surf lifesaver, contracted the virus from an infected prostitute and later developed the full-blown disease.

One of his last requests was to be allowed to return to his beachside home for a weekend.

But the overreaction of two ambulance officers to the danger the patient posed to them led to a personal disaster for the man who told friends he was dying of cancer.

Prof Dwyer said his friends had asked him if it was all-right to hold a surprise party for him.

"They said 10 or 15 of them would like to come and say goodbye," he said.

"It was a very sensitive sort of thing and I said, 'sure'. I thought he'd appreciate that.".

But when his friends saw him being carried on a stretcher by ambulance officers in "space suits" and kitchen gloves, they knew something was amiss.

"As soon as it was realised this man was infected, all of his friends who had come to say goodbye disappeared," Prof Dwyer said.

"That man died literally of a broken heart 48 hours later in my hospital."

TIME AND FRIENDSHIP

How many people have a news clipping framed in their house? I do, and maybe that makes me somewhat unusual. It is now an old story from an old newspaper in Melbourne, 'The Sun', now long gone, and I read it occasionally because I think it provides a good perspective about our common humanity. We think of news as something that can tell us about the world or about other people – but sometimes news can teach us something about ourselves as well.

The date 8 August 1988 might be one of vague mathematical curiosity (8-8-88) and yet it is etched into my mind as the day of a news report in which a young Sydney man lost his life, and yet his story continues to make me think and learn anew every time I stop to ponder its message.

The young man in question was infected with HIV in the days before modern multi-drug therapies made HIV a long-term medical condition instead of an almost-certain death sentence. His last request was to return home from hospital, and his friends eagerly organised a party for his return.

This was an era when HIV was greatly feared and stigmatised, in no small part due to its popular conflation with newly-decriminalised male homosexuality and imagined contagion through normal social contact. Accordingly, his ambulance attendants wore 'space suits' as they delivered him home on a stretcher. His friends fled when they saw this and realised that he had AIDS.

Doctor Julian Gold told the newspaper that the young man, 'died literally of a broken heart 48 hours later in my hospital'.

I was myself a young man when I read this story, and yet 33 years later, I remember being deeply touched by this tale of abandonment by mates and friends. We all recall the flush of youth and our eagerness to find special friends and share time and companionship with those who share our youthful enthusiasm for living and loving and learning together. This is part of the natural process of maturation, moving beyond close family, in search of our own more individualised, extended family. In his desire to find significance and belonging among his own friends – and in their failure to meet his expectations – this young man's story touches something primal in us all. (Wherever they are today, I hope that his friends have learnt from their past mistake – we are all only human, after all – and have gone on to redress their error of having been less than their best when the going got tough).

We might also learn something from the yearning for companionship within his story – our common human condition means that we share a bond with others, regardless of their age, gender, culture, sexuality, or any other marker that has traditionally been used to separate and divide us. We share the ability to hope and dream; to yearn for significance and betterment; for living and laughing and crying. Like all sentient beings, we share the potential for suffering or flourishing, for intimacy or loneliness.

Whether they may be runaway or refugee, indigenous or ill, disempowered or discriminated against – our sentience surely compels us to empathise with others in need, and go out of our way to support them whenever we can. Indeed, I suspect that the fullest test of our humanity, ethics and compassion is whether or not we help those with whom we might ordinarily feel that we share the *least* in common, except for our common humanity.

I am reminded of a Biblical injunction to sacrificially offer help to others: *Greater love hath no man than he who gives his life for his friends.* I see this saying immortalised on war memorials, building plaques, tomb stones, and used ubiquitously across common literature. However, I see deficiencies in this quote; after all, even serial killers and dictators care about their friends; and its wording suggests an elitism by implying that only friends are worth protecting rather than all humanity. I would respectfully amend and supersede this Biblical quote, emphasising its secular humanist ideal and removing it from any religious context, by expanding it to include everyone instead of just an insulated bubble of our nearest and dearest: *Greater love hath no person than they who give their life to help another; turning strangers and enemies and their whole human family into friends.*

Thirty-three years ago, that anonymous young man's story convinced me that awareness of the suffering of others is our choice. His story inspired me towards activism. *How many others are like him today, around the world, suffering in silence during modern-day plagues: HIV, COVID, disease, poverty, starvation, injustice, war, violence, discrimination, or the indifference of others? And what are we doing about it?*

However we answer those questions reveals more about our own humanity than it does about those whose suffering we are challenged to confront.

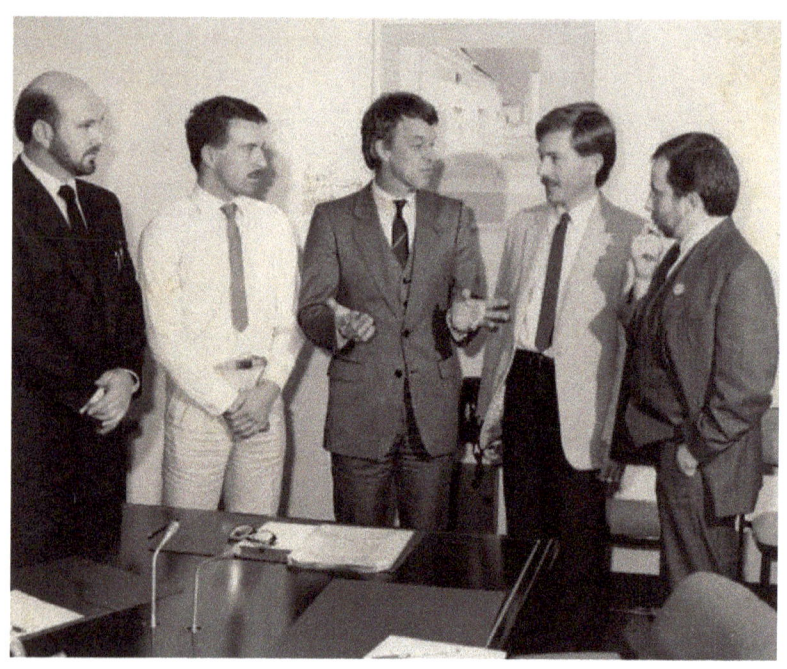

Dr Neal Blewett, Federal Minister for Health (middle) and gay community AIDS leaders (L-R Bill Rutkin (Qld), Peter Loddon (AFOA Exec Officer), Greg Tillett (NSW) and Phil Carswell (Vic)

Postcard, 1993. David McDiarmid (1952-1995). From collection of Henry von Doussa

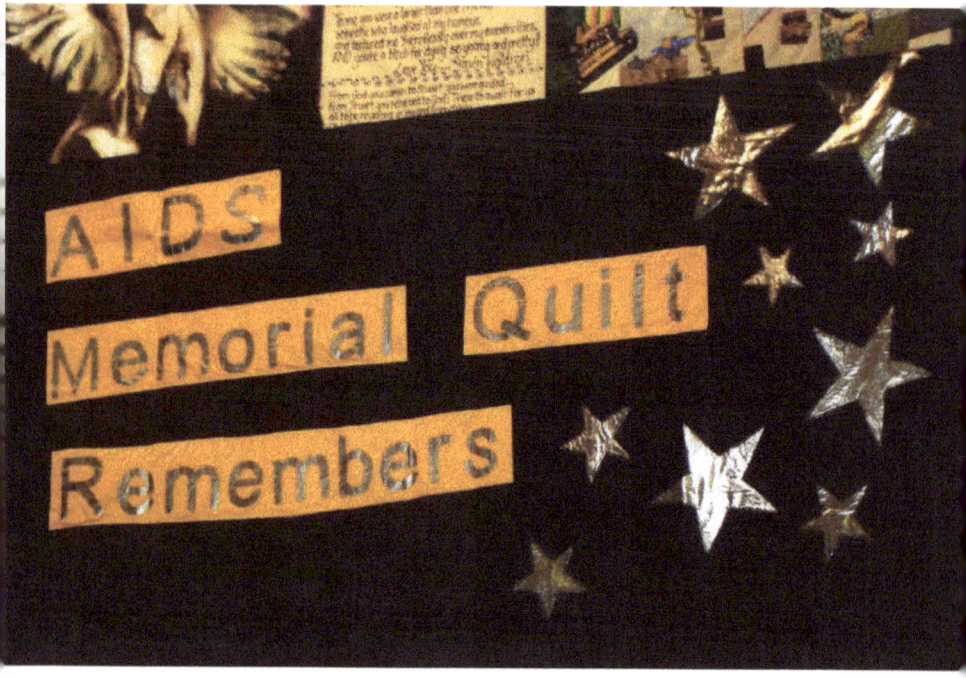

Quilt banner. Geoff Allshorn

FILM

Lockdowns from COVID-19 have hit the cinema industry hard, and many people have not been to the movies for quite some time (even allowing for modern trends in home cinema etc).

For me, COVID has made little difference. The lack of LGBT representation in films has discouraged me from going to the movies for many years, although recent US movies such as Behind the Candelabra (2013) *and* United in Anger (2012) *have increasingly broken with this tradition and featured stories of HIV/AIDS.*

If only the Aussie film industry was also willing to give a fair go to the HIV/AIDS underdog.

In the 1994 Australian film, *The Sum of Us*, single father Harry Mitchell is incapacitated by a stroke and is cared for by his young gay son, Jeff. In a moment of candid disclosure, Harry confesses his fears for his son through an oblique reference to 'that dreadful disease'. The word 'AIDS' is not spoken, but its contemporaneous association with gay men was so commonly understood in Australia at the time, that this reference to (rewording Oscar Wilde) an affliction that dare not speak its name was immediately understood by Australian audiences. Nowadays, that same quote may require translation for a new generation.

Two other mainstream Australian films from the time can be found which reference AIDS. In *The Adventures of Priscilla, Queen of the Desert* (1994), the bus Priscilla is vandalised with AIDS-phobic graffiti. *Walking on Water* (2003) begins with the death of a gay man whose circumstances are immediately recognisable to those affected by AIDS. However, both films pointedly fail to explore the affliction in any explicit way, thereby providing obtuse allusions to some unmentionable mortality.

It might be argued that such movies follow the formulaic

slew of American telemovies and films that perpetuated what Vito Russo, author of *The Celluloid Closet,* asserted as the Hollywood archetype by portraying gay men as the 'other'. The most famous US AIDS movie during the era of AIDS was *Philadelphia* (1993), which starred heterosexual actor, Tom Hanks, presenting his character in a way that 'even a straight audience would understand'. Heterosexual families, mothers or carers were often the unsung heroes of these US movies because the wholesome, soft, maternal female archetype was apparently more palatable for Hollywood than the diseased, stigmatised gay male. In Australia, that representation of 'otherness' was so extreme as to virtually ethnically cleanse those with AIDS from our films altogether.

Even the 1988 Australian-New Zealand film, *The Navigator: A Medieval Odyssey* featuring the medieval plague and transporting Cumbrian villagers to a modern-day city, included an oblique allusion to HIV/AIDS (The Grim Reaper TV ad), However, once again, the link was not made explicit.

Thus we see a tradition of writing AIDS *out* of our popular cultural representations. While activists and historians praise Australia's historically low HIV infection rates and attribute this to an early history of collaboration between government agencies and activists, our nation has a long and troubled history of denial about HIV/AIDS. In considering how AIDS may have affected people in the 1980s and 1990s, historians should be mindful that Australian films have largely excluded HIV-positive people for forty years, and this absence speaks volumes for those living with the virus. The 2015 film, *Holding the Man*, was a welcome, modern exception to this tradition.

The invisibility, chaos and confusion of the early 1980s can be clearly seen reflected in the media hysteria of the early days of AIDS. It was not uncommon to open a newspaper and read hysterical headlines such as, 'Die You Deviate!' or,

'Mosquitoes can carry AIDS virus'. Amidst such popular representations, the individual AIDS patient remained an elusive and largely invisible character, contextualised by taboo and marginalisation. Once Australia's panic died down and heterosexual people realised they were not in a high-risk group, AIDS appeared to effectively go 'underground'.

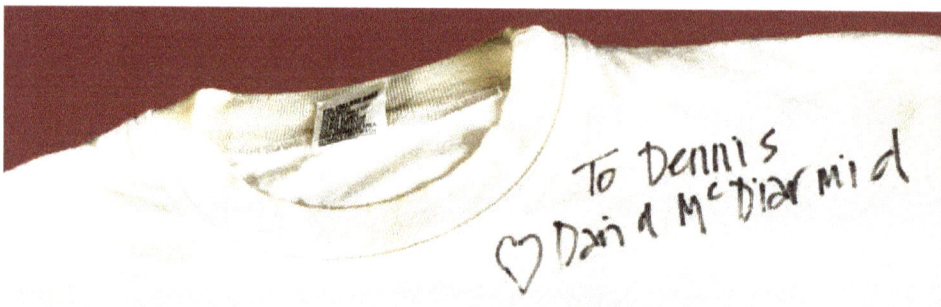

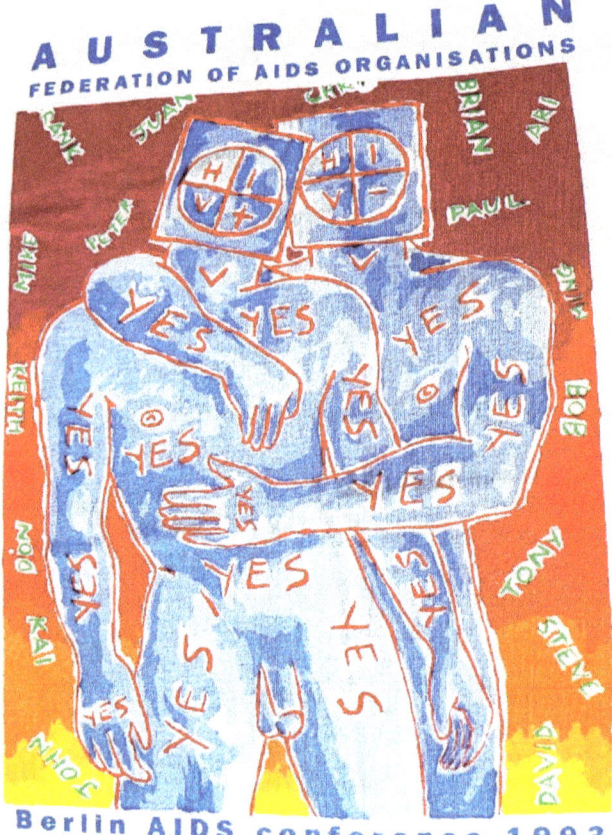

T-shirt, signed by artist David McDiarmid. Picture, Dennis Altman

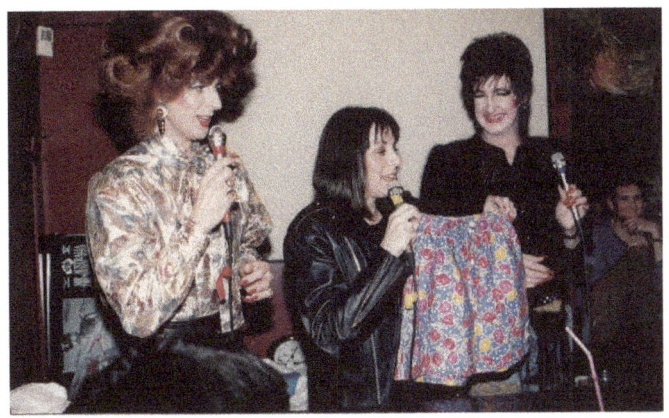

One of many The Laird fundraisers. Denise Drysdale (centre). Phil Carswell.

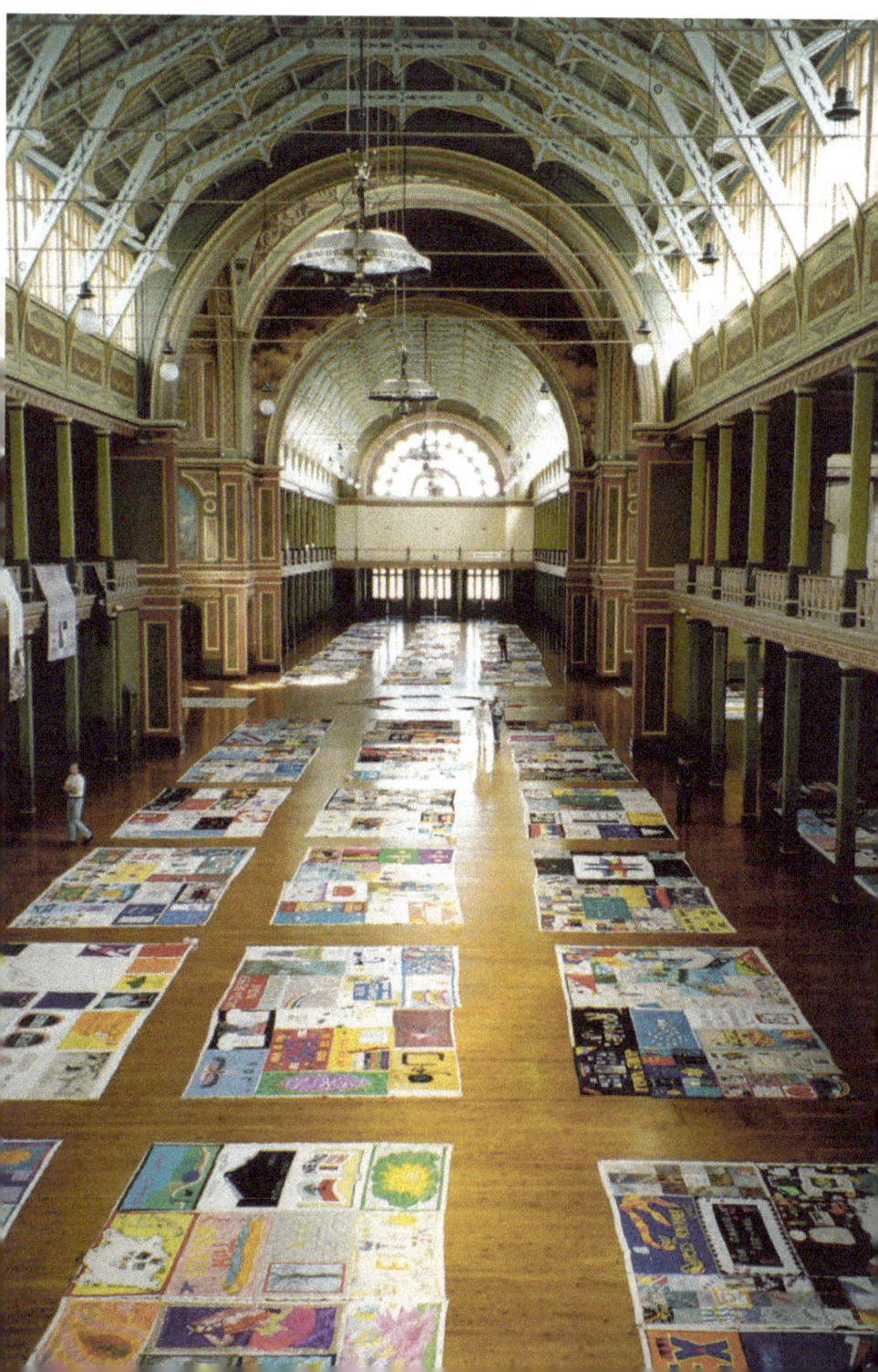

AND A CHILD SHALL LEAD

The 1994 AIDS Quilt memorial in the Exhibition Buildings was a silent, sombre and moving affair. As curious or grieving crowds entered the building and respectfully gathered alongside quilts to study, mourn and maybe remember their lost loved ones, I became aware of a family group that was standing at one block of panels. A little girl pointed to a panel and said excitedly, 'Look Mummy, there's Daddy's quilt!' All the gathered adults standing alongside, in the crowd, silently turned their gaze to look at the panel she was pointing towards. It contained a family photo of a young father with wife and children, including this young girl. Immediately and silently, every adult in the gathered crowd looked away to hide their tears.

< opposite AIDS Quilt memorial in the Royal Exhibition Building, Meblourne, 1999. Geoff Allsohorn

Given the dearth of educational material relating to AIDS for children, there were some attempts to introduce related profound topics in matter-of-fact and age-appropriate ways.

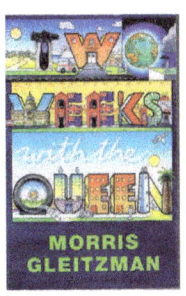

Two Weeks with the Queen by Morris Gleitzman, Pan Macmillan, 1990 (various reprints).

Australian author Morris Gleitzman added his moral support to the cause with this addition to his impressive collection of children's books. The story features a boy who travels to London to meet the Queen but instead meets a gay man who teaches him about life and death with AIDS – and about the value of family. This story undoubtedly helped to introduce AIDS and gay people to many thousands of young readers. The book was also turned into a play.

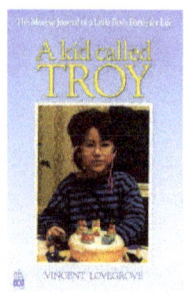

A Kid Called Troy by Vince Lovegrove, ABC Books, 1993.

Son of Vince and Suzi Lovegrove ('Suzi's Story'), young Troy Lovegrove was the subject of a book and a TV documentary ('A Kid Called Troy'), passing away shortly before his eighth birthday in 1993. 'When I die, I want all the poor children to have my toys and my clothes.' As a eulogy, the book contains a poem written by his sister, Holly.

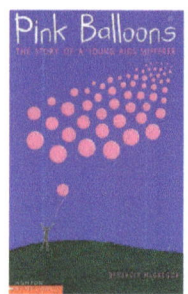

Pink Balloons: The Story of A Young AIDS Sufferer by Beverley McGregor, Ashton Scholastic, 1995.

Blood transfusion recipient Skye Bussenschutt received an AIDS diagnosis just a week after her fifth birthday. 'I want someone to write a book about me so everyone can know what it's like to live with AIDS. I don't want to be forgotten'. After her death in 1992, her school friends released pink balloons.

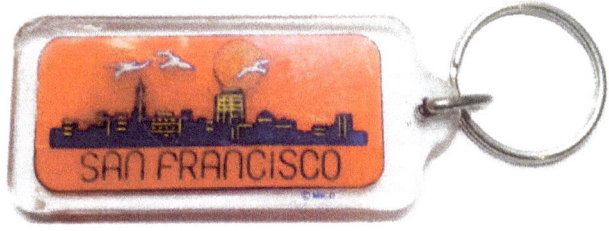

keyring from San Francisco circa 1990. Geoff Allshorn

A TALE OF TWO CITIES

I still have a key ring from San Francisco – a souvenir from my partner when he visited the city around 1990. It is a utilitarian object, if maybe in a garish colour, and it is now somewhat battered from indeterminate use over subsequent years To him, it was a minor souvenir from his visit to a gay mecca. To me, it was a somewhat exotic trinket from a far-away place that we knew was being plagued with AIDS. Sometimes nowadays, I ponder this object and think of the many young men (and others) who were lost around the time that the keyring was on sale perhaps in some hippie market or gay venue. The simple item sits silently in my house today, and says nothing of the lives and losses it may have witnessed as carnage ravaged The City. Silence speaks volumes.

In 1988, a mere seven years into the epidemic, the Mayor of San Francisco told the US Presidential Commission on AIDS that his city had already lost more young men to AIDS than it had to World Wars I and II, Korea and Vietnam – combined and doubled.

The arrival of HIV/AIDS in the 1980s transformed both San Francisco and Melbourne. While the USA and Australia were still formulating their national, political and cultural responses to HIV/AIDS – responses that would at times include hysteria, fear, stigma, vilification and discrimination – it was the gay communities that led the fightback, which they defined within the context of saving lives, caring for the sick, celebrating diversity and promoting gay rights.

San Francisco and Melbourne can be seen to share some historic and social intersections. Both are locations in relatively affluent 'western' democracies which were originally inhabited by indigenous peoples who were later dispossessed by white European colonizers; both cities received a boost in economy and population from the mid-19th century Gold Rush; and both places are now seen as centres of culturally and linguistically diverse communities.

While Melbourne was traditionally viewed by many as a city where much of its culture appeared to stop upon six o'clock closing, its post-war immigration encouraged the evolution of a more cosmopolitan, multicultural society. Meanwhile, San Francisco was popularly known as a centre for bohemian culture. In 1950, legal protections for gay people were already being established by law in San Francisco, while this did not commence in Melbourne until the decriminalisation of homosexuality in 1980. In the 1960s, Scott McKenzie was encouraging people to join the hippie counter-culture by travelling to San Francisco – and 'be sure to wear a flower in your hair'. In the 1970s, the Village People encouraged young gay men to 'Go West' and to join the gay community of San Francisco because 'life is peaceful there'. Tragically, this drawing together into a close-knit community may have provided a locus for a new viral agent.

Both cities became a destination for an influx of young gay men who were seeking escape from oppressive country towns, as fictionalised in San Francisco's Tales of the City books by Armistead Maupin. San Franscisco's gay culture was epitomised by Harvey Milk and civil rights activism. By contrast, I have been told by gay men that they socialised in Melbourne's gay venues on weekends and then went and lived more closeted lives at home and work.

In November 1980, a gay man named Ken visited his doctor's office in San Francisco and was diagnosed with Kaposi's sarcoma, a type of cancer connected with AIDS, and he would later become the first officially registered Person With AIDS (Stryker and Van Buskirk, 1996, 85 & 86). His life and death are documented, along with those of other early protagonists in the fight against AIDS from San Francisco and New York City, in Randy Shilt's study *And the Band Played On*. It is reported that by 1989, almost half of the gay men over age 26 in San Francisco were infected with HIV (Rodgers et al, 1995, 669) and that by 1995, the city had the highest per capita infection rate of any city in the USA as well as the highest percentage of AIDS-related deaths (1.7%)' (ibid, 666).

In December 1981, young Bobbi Campbell from San Francisco publicly disclosed his status as a person living with Kaposi's Sarcoma. He created a poster about 'Gay Cancer' which he placed in a pharmacy window (Stryker and Van Buskirk, 1996, 86 & 87.) Campbell was one of the first gay men to attempt to seize control of his situation and agitate for public education and action. We can see the start of local activism that would affect not only San Franciscans but also have an international impact. San Francisco not only served as a place where local conditions – in this case, a large collectivised gay community – would provide one locus for an infective agent; the city also demonstrated that epidemics – and human responses to such epidemics – could ebb and flow into and out of localised geographical centres and travel the world.

San Francisco received no prior warning of AIDS, and by the time they rallied, many people had already been lost. By contrast, Melbourne's gay community received warnings in advance, and they had time to develop community support networks and distribute information. There are no statistics available on the estimated number of gay men living in Melbourne in the 1980s or 1990s due to the covert nature of homosexuality at the time and due to the absence of a strongly united gay community as there had been in San Francisco. Statistics do show that in the early 1980s, hundreds of gay men were diagnosed annually with HIV/AIDS (Author unknown, 1999).

At the 25th anniversary of the Victorian AIDS Council, founding President Phil Carswell recalled the dread and apprehension which they all felt back in those early days and their inability to fully grasp the gravity of the coming problem: *'Looking ahead, we thought we could see a tsunami was coming. What we failed to understand was that it wasn't a tsunami; it was a whole climate change'* (Carswell, 2009).

In 1983, when Australia's first AIDS fatality occurred in Melbourne, the story appeared on page 3 of *The San Francisco Chronicle* (United Press, 1983). Its prominence in this newspaper might suggest that the patient – known to have lived in the USA for some years – may have had friends in San Francisco – or that gay community links between the two cities were strong enough to warrant this news being placed in prominent position in the Bay City.

A number of comparisons could be made between community responses in San Francisco and Melbourne, and this is the first and most obvious: in San Francisco, the Kaposi's Sarcoma Foundation was started in April 1982 and was later to be renamed the San Francisco AIDS Foundation (SFAF, 2012); while in Melbourne, the Victorian AIDS Action Committee was founded in July 1983, later renamed the Victorian AIDS Council. Both organisations were started by coalitions of gay activists and doctors, and both were born out of a groundswell of community concern. There was open liaison between both cities.

The San Francisco model of health care became somewhat of a template for the Melbourne response. This 'model' encompassed medical staff, carers and volunteers working collaboratively in every aspect of patient care and treatment, including collaborating closely with local community organisations. This included the emergent, grass-roots volunteer care teams and other support structures; thousands of hours of volunteer work from both homosexual and heterosexual people, possibly the first time that so many volunteers had rallied to confront an epidemic.

Randy Shilts wrote of this model in 1992:

The importance of San Francisco General Hospital in the history of the AIDS epidemic cannot be overstated. The model of care now used the world over was pioneered in those buildings. (Shilts, 1992, ix and x.)

Fairfield Hospital in Melbourne was also a centre of medical excellence and innovation, one of synergy between doctors and activists; a place where patients became self-empowered to define and determine their own treatment options (Allshorn, 2011). Although it was closed in 1996, the hospital's legacy is a paradigm of collaborative discourse between patients and doctors.

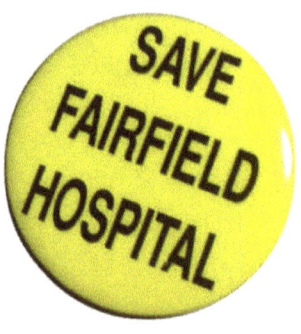

When we look at both cities, we can see differences emerge even when close correlation is apparent: the SFAF expanded its services to assist affected cohorts, including gay men, injecting drug users, women, and CALD communities (SFAF, 2021). By contrast, the VAC focussed its work predominantly on gay men. This may reflect differing social hierarchies in these cities: San Francisco's gay community had enjoyed greater civil rights, whereas Melbourne's gay community was more covert and emergent, and evidently saw a need to establish their own exclusive support structures.

Strangely, the activism in both cities may have been energised by converse governmental responses to HIV/AIDS. In the USA, Ronald Reagan became President in 1981, just as AIDS was being discovered. Many commentators criticise his failure to significantly address AIDS as a public health issue for the first seven years of his eight year administration. Suggested one critic: 'Ronald Reagan cared more about UFOs than AIDS' (Pareene, 2011). The San Francisco Mayor stated in 1988 that: 'What threatens to overwhelm San Francisco is not the increased caseload of AIDS, but the continued lack of leadership from the federal government.' (Krohn, 1988).

In Australia, our federal government took steps to work cooperatively with affected communities in order to develop effective responses to the epidemic (Carswell, 1986). This meant that unlike San Francisco, where the activist community was forced into activism due to the inaction of their national government, Melbourne's activists were being empowered by governmental recognition. Despite somewhat tangential political actuation, both cities achieved a similar result and created a powerful local activist movement.

Community activism in both cities did include forms of protest. The group ACT UP (AIDS Coalition to Unleash Power) was a radical protest group founded in New York City to fight for those with AIDS, particularly to demand their access to potentially life-saving drugs. Chapters of ACT UP formed around the world. ACT UP Melbourne was enthusiastic but short-lived, perhaps lacking the rage of their US counterparts because of our more collaborative government.

AIDS memorial rituals were also developed in San Francisco and exported to the world. These include Candlelight Vigils, starting in San Francisco in 1983 and continuing to this day (SFAF, 2012). Melbourne's Candlelight Vigil has almost disappeared in recent years. Similarly, San Francisco boasts a National AIDS Memorial Grove, while Melbourne's AIDS Gardens remain largely forgotten.

The AIDS Quilt, created by San Francisco gay activist Cleve Jones in 1987, remains available for display across the USA, while most of Australia's AIDS Quilt is now stored in a

Sydney museum, and Melbourne – perhaps surprisingly – boasted its longest surviving chapter. These varied outcomes demonstrate that even when community activism is directly transmitted by human and cultural interaction, the resulting outcomes are reliant upon local conditions and personalities.

Rodgers et al assert that 'When a major event threatens the stability of a system, it forces the members of the system to construct new and changing meanings of their community.' They also suggest that HIV/AIDS reconstructed the social fabric of San Francisco (Rodgers et al, 1995, 676). Dennis Altman has called for greater acknowledgement that HIV/AIDS has contributed to the development of Australia's modern gay community. My study demonstrates the complexities faced by trans-national communities even when they are facing a similar problem or share some cultural antecedents and aspirations. This comparison also shows the ability of local communities to develop their own systems of self-empowerment and to adapt templates to suit local needs when facing challenging times. Such a template might be adapted to suit local conditions in other places.

The world needs to learn lessons from this history because there will be another time, another place and another epidemic. Cleve Jones recalls that the SFAF's phone started to ring before they had even advertised its existence. He evokes a universal symbolism for local activist communities everywhere: 'The phone never stopped ringing. Thirty years later, it's still ringing' (SFAF, 2012).

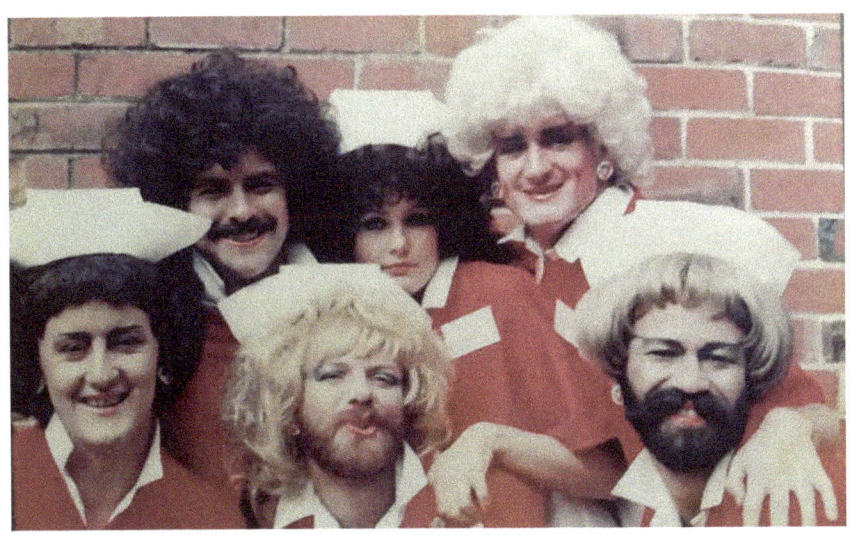

Safe-Sex Sisters. Picture, Phil Carswell

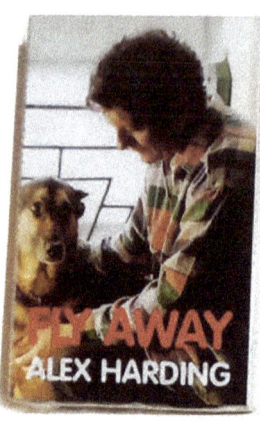
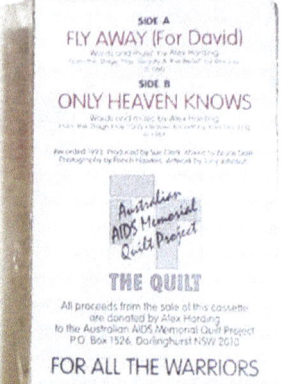

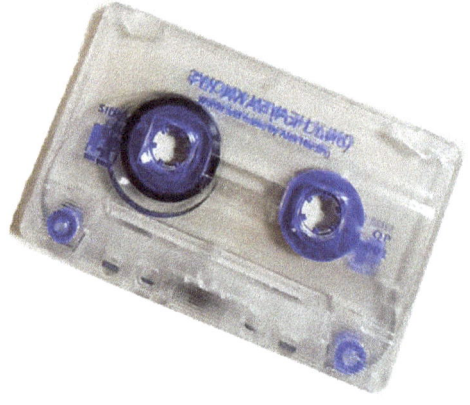

MAKING MUSIC

Fly Away Cassette

Two songs from his own original material by playwright Alec Harding were collected on a cassette to raise money for the Australian AIDS Memorial Quilt chapter based in Darlinghurst, Sydney. A review of one of his source plays later suggested that: '*Only heaven knows* premiered at a time when HIV/AIDS was sweeping across the world, and bringing with it great hostility towards the gay community. At that time, this story promoting the need for tolerance and compassion would have certainly packed a punch.'

Voices For Life CD (1993)

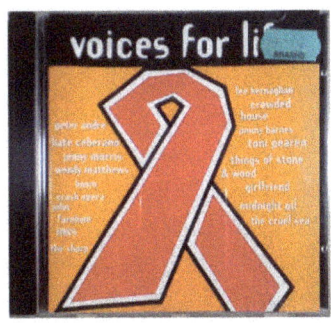

A compilation CD of well-known musicians (including John Farnham, Kate Ceberano, INXS, Jimmy Barnes, Midnight Oil and Crowded House) collected together into a fund-raising CD for the AIDS Trust of Australia. Chairman of the Trust, Ita Buttrose, thanked the musicians on behalf of 'all of us dedicated to beating HIV/AIDS' and spoke of the priorities in HIV/AIDS for the coming years, where no cure was in sight: home care, research, and public education.

PRICS CD (October 1996)

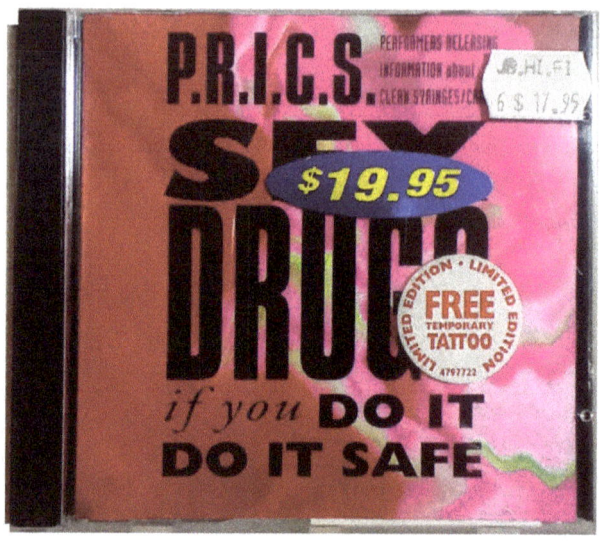

'Performers Releasing Information about Clean Syringes/Careful Sex' was a group of musicians who sought to educate audiences about HIV/AIDS and other STDs. This CD was financed by a grant from the Commonwealth Department of Human Services and Health, manufactured and distributed by EMI for the Australian Broadcasting Corporation, Triple J and Virgin Records. A free temporary tattoo was included featuring a safe sex snake. Clearly designed for a target audience that preferred edgier material than the 'top ten' play list, the CD featured songs such as 'Sex, Drugs (If you do it, do it safe)', 'Sexuality', and 'Pretend That We're Dead'.

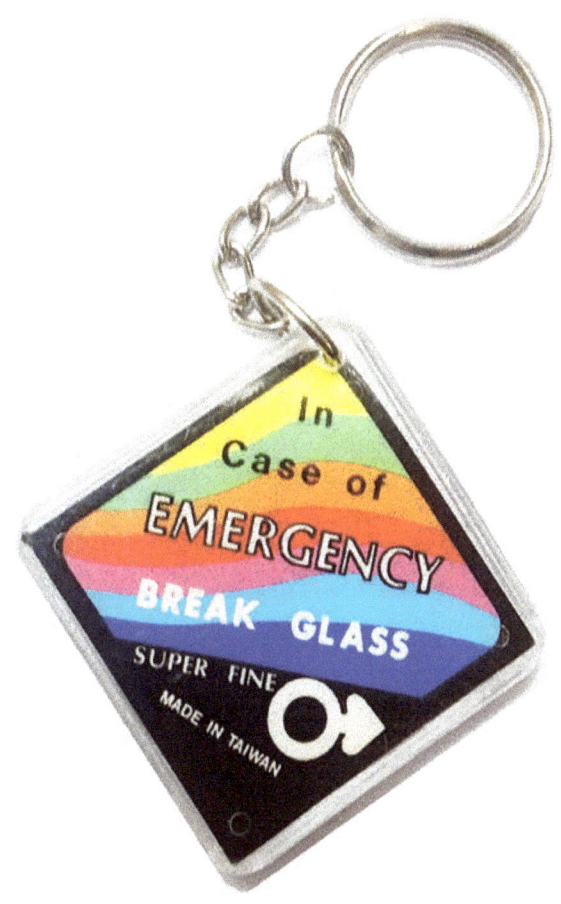

Keyring includes condom

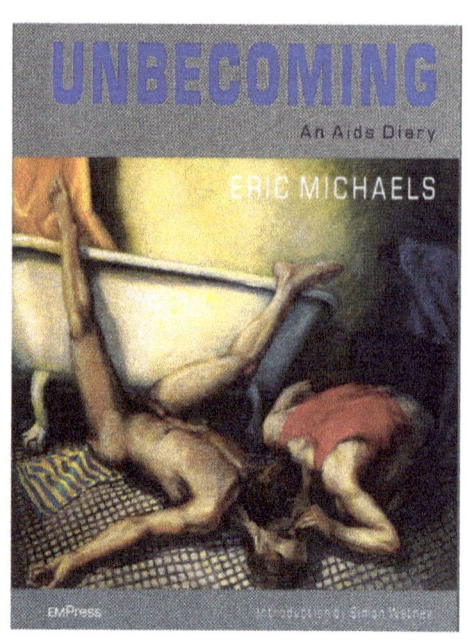

BECOMING

My introduction to Eric Michaels' book Unbecoming *was when I sought out a copy in a prominent public library. Upon my request, the book was duly collected from the stacks and delivered to me – missing its colourful cover, which appeared to have been removed with surgical precision along the edge of its spine. When I asked the librarian what happened to the book, he carelessly shrugged. I later purchased another copy of the book online and donated it to the same public library, so that Eric Michaels' words would be available to the public in the exact condition that he would have wanted.*

If one is going to go to all the trouble to be gay, one ought to do a more interesting and useful job of it. Models exist in our very recent past. They should be recalled. – Eric Michaels, 1990b, 192.

The words of Eric Michaels speak to us from the days of a terrible epidemic – one that was perceived to target people who were disempowered, stigmatised, invisible, and/or socially undesirable. At a time of terrible stigma, discrimination and open homophobia, Michaels encouraged the gay community to find role models and create its own pride amidst the prejudice. In doing so, he became one of those role models.

Stigma and invisibility continue today, in that the AIDS epidemic remains largely overlooked and forgotten.

The Australian Dictionary of Biography reports that Eric Michaels was born in 1948 to Jewish parents in Philadelphia, USA, and became a hippie studying cultural anthropology, examining groups as disparate as Christian fundamentalists in Texas, USA, and the Yanomami people of Brazil. He arrived in Australia in 1982 and ultimately became a lecturer at Griffith University in Brisbane, dying with AIDS in 1988. (Cunningham, 2012)

A tragic coincidence of timing meant that he arrived in Australia at approximately the same time as another US import: a particular strain of HIV and AIDS. Michaels thereby became somewhat of a potential double outcast: disapproved in mainstream Australia because he was gay, and also socially isolated from some sections within the Australian gay community because he was American in the days when the origin of AIDS was attributed to gay Americans (and well might we learn from his experience today, during another pandemic, when some people seek to scapegoat others from another country where COVID is meant to have originated – as though its geographic origin has anything significant to do with its treatment or mitigation). Paul Foss notes that 'Eric's sense of personal loss and betrayal' – at his rejection at least as much as his actual AIDS mortality – contributed to an 'accusatory tone' as well as 'venom and impish humour' in his writing (Foss, 1990, 13). In harnessing and harvesting this anger, Michaels foreshadows the rise of ACT-UP, an activist group borne of self-empowerment and anger.

For Eric Michaels, it is likely that this 'otherness' may have contributed to his writing/publishing his AIDS diary in the days before any Australian gay man had the interest or opportunity to do so. Those early days saw women such as Suzi Lovegrove take that same opportunity to bypass the dominant homophobic prejudice against the epidemic in Australia and create autobiographical documentation, such as the film, *Suzi's Story*, or varied biographies. Michaels' diary was the earliest such effort from a gay man to break out of what he termed the 'lavender prison' of homophobia (Michaels 1990b, 191).

It also seems probable that this 'otherness' similarly motivated Eric Michaels to spend much of his professional life assisting similarly disempowered voices. His academic career in Australia had revolved around, 'empowering

Aborigines through the appropriation of new technology' (Cunningham, 2012) and he had asserted that, 'a cultural future can only result from political resistance' (Michaels, 1987, 78). And yet he was also very conscious of the 'politics of speech' in empowering the very voices he wished to highlight (O'Regan, 1990; see also Michaels 1994).

Such empowerment foreshadowed the empowerment of indigenous and other voices during the AIDS epidemic; from gay men to women and others who fought for their lives as well as their civil rights. Their battle resonates a generation later, after male homosexuality has been decriminalised and destigmatised, in no small part due to these foot soldiers.

Michael's situation and perspective seem to echo those of his contemporary, Scottish journalist and New Zealand resident Tom Maclean, whose own AIDS pathography, *If I Should Die: Living With AIDS*, reflects the life and times of his trans-Tasman gay compatriot. Whereas Michaels implicitly evokes a firm resolution to choose life and activism, McLean more pointedly speaks about this stark choice among the last words in his own book, which was published four days before his death in 1989 at age 40 (PA, 1989). 'There's a lesson in everything if you look for it,' McLean writes, 'Even in AIDS' (McLean, 1989, 98).

His friend John Hobson eulogised Michaels with recollections of their life and times together, but spoke frankly about his last photograph:

'The last image of Eric shows the ravages of Kaposi's Sarcoma; a rare form of skin cancer prevalent in the early years of the epidemic. It is almost unheard of these days thanks to advances in treatments. It is definitely a shocking image, but one that Eric chose to be published as his final one. As well as a clinical photo to evidence his ultimate reality, it was also clearly one last opportunity for him to poke his tongue out at the world.' Hobson, n.d (b).

Hobson also notes that after his death, Eric Michaels' Warlpiri and Kardiya friends from Yuendumu created an AIDS Quilt memorial panel in his memory. (Hobson, n.d.(b).)

The title of his diary, *Unbecoming*, is a play on words: tapping into the societal disapproval of gay men as being somewhat unbecoming, it also implicitly examines his own unravelling life due to AIDS and questions whether he is, in some inverse act of creation, literally un-becoming himself. Ultimately, he demonstrates that in his becoming less or other than himself, he is also becoming much more – perhaps the perfect symbolism for an activist seeking to create something positive out of loss. A generation later, as the world seeks to rebuild or redefine itself after the ravages of another pandemic, we might learn valuable lessons from this experience.

Although written during the era of AIDS, Michaels' words resonate during our era of COVID:

Maybe the lunatic right wing will mobilise and we will have to drag ourselves out of this languor to protect ourselves and respond. Or maybe the baby boom will eventually reach their sixties and, upon looking back, develop a more powerful criticism than any advanced so far. (Michaels, 1990b, 192).

Maybe.

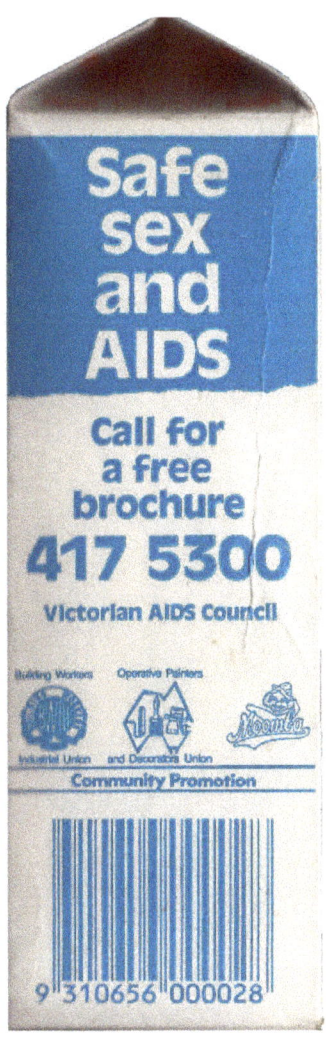

VicAIDS milk carton with AIDS Awareness message produced by Moomba and Vic Trades Hall Council. Phil Carswell

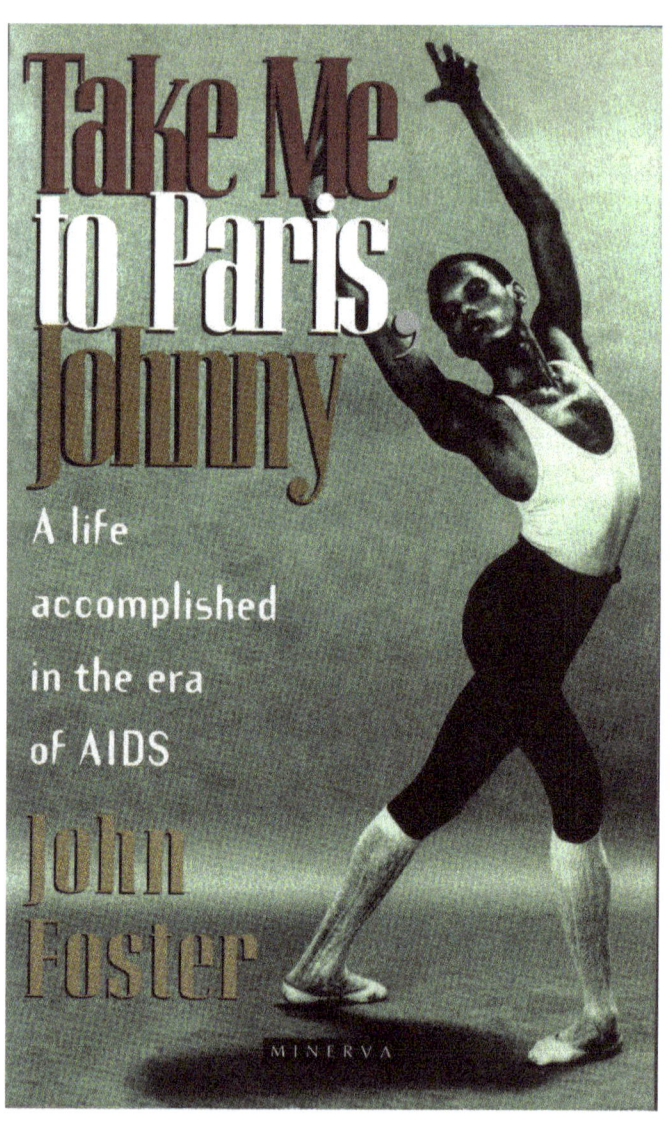

Take Me to Paris, Johnny

A life
accomplished
in the era
of AIDS

John Foster

MINERVA

DO YOU REMEMBER

In 1993, Minerva Books published a memoir written by Melbourne academic John Foster, which immortalised the life and death of his partner. A generation later, we are experiencing another pandemic, and this book – *Take Me To Paris, Johnny* – subsequently reissued by Black Inc. in 2003 and most recently in 2016 by the Text Publishing Company, is something of an overlooked classic. Given its literary merit – Peter Craven (1994) praises this writing as 'unparalleled in Australian letters' – it is surprising that John Foster's book has not received wider acclamation.

The answer, it seems, might be found in the historical context of the times. A generation has now passed since the arrival of AIDS, and much of our societal ignorance, fear and hysteria have dissolved into the calm of complacency. AIDS, which was once loudly denounced everywhere from pulpit to Parliament, has instead succumbed to the ultimate stigma: that of being generally forgotten and invisible. Foster's novel is both a victim of, and a challenge against, such invisibility. It reminds us that HIV/AIDS is still here – and that we are greatly diminished when we overlook the courage of its heroes.

Take Me To Paris, Johnny is the real-life story of Juan Céspedes, the Cuban refugee and US emigre who arrives in Melbourne in 1986 to begin a new life filled with love, cautious hope and limited possibilities – only to be struck down with AIDS. Foster's affectionate testimony to Juan's resilience transforms the young man into the human personification of John Donne's call for compassion: 'Any man's death diminishes me, because I am involved in Mankind ...' Juan's Cuban mother and grandmother – whose distant lives interweave a mixture of both compassion and heartbreaking tragedy – are also transformed by Foster into figures who, through their suffering and loss, are evocative of the mother of Jesus. Such religious allusion subtly enriches Foster's writing at different times throughout the novel.

Foster's devout religious convictions might puzzle anyone who believes the term 'gay Christian' to be potentially oxymoronic – even more so in the 1980s, when religious-based vilification was aimed at many people with AIDS. Such contradictions, however, are apparently not unusual for John Foster: an administrator who hates bureaucracy (Robertson, 1994) and an academic who falls in love with a self-educated dancer. Most paradoxically, Foster is an historian who teaches his students about the horrors of the Holocaust whilst conceding in his book that history holds a callous disregard for mere mortals: 'Mostly it neither absolves nor condemns; it simply forgets'. Like his teaching, Foster's personal memoir is a protest against such oblivion – this latter being a tribute to his partner, Juan, whose deathbed exclamation of heartbreaking despair, 'I have accomplished nothing', sparks Foster's determination to document his life and death (Rickard, 2003).

The story is large and literate in scope, evocative even of a Shakespearean epic. Foster's star-crossed lovers battle both society's disapproval of their relationship and a deadlier 'plague on both their houses'. Whereas Shakespeare's fictional characters die in suicidal despair, Foster's real-life lovers find consolation within their relationship: 'We made it, Johnny. Didn't we?'

John and Juan's relationship can also be seen as an Australian story because it is the embodiment of multiculturalism and diversity. Their potentially intergenerational partnership – common enough in the gay community (Wilde, 2008) – is complicated by differences of race, education, class, culture and language. Foster nevertheless demonstrates unconditional love and acceptance, for example by accepting Juan's infidelities either by choosing wilful ignorance or through a dismissive attitude akin to 'boys will be boys'. Such is the nature of their unconventional partnership; one which some religions might propound as being symptomatic of the 'sinful' nature of homosexuality, but which Foster, as a Christian, presents without apology or reservation – his is neither a tale of political activism nor moral turpitude (Dessaix 1994), but simply a narration exposing a facet of what he considers to be real life.

Despite this implicit documentation of 'ordinariness', Foster's writing also resonates with his personal sense of 'otherness' as revealed in his earlier book about WW2 German Jewish refugees when he summarises the effects of war, flight as refugees and subsequent cultural assimilation: 'In Melbourne, German Jews have ceased to be a community … It is the memory of a past which is proud, terrible and still problematic' (Foster, 1986). Such mixed feelings and fears are reflected in *Take Me To Paris, Johnny* when Juan's difficulties as a refugee and a gay man with AIDS allude to the plight of 'pariahs' within Australian society (Baker 1994); they imply a concern by Foster that AIDS might decimate his own gay family just as life's harsh realities ravaged members of the German Jewish community.

There may even be a further parallel concerning the struggle within Foster's own faith as a gay Christian, a minority within a minority which was under attack from both disease and discrimination. It may indeed be John Foster's very underlying assumption – that gay men can find acceptance and love within the religious community – which has contributed to the avoidance of this text by some Australian readers.

Juan's more obvious 'otherness' exposes different possible interpretations of his life and motivations. Readers might criticise Juan for relying on the financial support of older men in order to compensate for his own lifelong failure to forge a successful career for himself (Dessaix, 1994). A more benign interpretation might see Juan as someone who strives to improve his lot (Hanrahan, 2003) but upon whom fate inflicts many cruelties – until he is blessed through the friendship of John Foster. Williams (1994) evokes this latter alternative in his character description of Juan: 'attractively elegant, talented, flawed, and unlucky in just about everything, except his choice of lovers.'

As an example of the fickleness of fate, Juan lies dying just as the 'Grim Reaper' campaign is terrorising Australian television in 1987, and this fills Foster with impotent rage. After all, the faceless 'other' who is being publicly vilified as someone to fear is none other than gentle Juan. In the end, it matters not whatever might form the course or cause of Juan's life journey; readers are uplifted by the end of his vigil when he discovers the redemptive power of love.

'Who, in their right mind, would actually want to read a book ... about AIDS?' – apparently wrote one reviewer of an early New Zealand AIDS anthology, and was soundly criticised for this comment by Tom McLean, a Scottish journalist who was living and dying in New Zealand at around the same time as the characters in Foster's book. McLean wrote his own AIDS autobiography, *If I Should Die: Living With AIDS*, dying three days after its publication (Young, 2002?a) – departing this life, like Juan Céspedes, on a Good Friday (Young, 2002?b).

The vexed question remains: 'Who would want to read a book about AIDS?' – particularly in this decade when AIDS is seen as being barely newsworthy. Perhaps the answer is obvious: Everyone, because in learning about John and Juan, we are learning about ourselves.

Indeed, why did the world find Anne Frank's diary about the Holocaust to be so compelling and personal? Both Anne

Frank and Juan Céspedes share a childlike optimism despite imminent disaster; moreover, both their testimonies resonate with a mix of inner personal voices and external human truths which echo Walt Whitman's decree: 'I am large, I contain multitudes'.

Robin Grove (1994/1995) observes another parallel in Foster's book: 'JUAN is JOHN, John Juan, each in the language of the other ...' and this is the first of many parallels within and without the memoir. Juan receives almost identical care at the start and end of his life; his compassion for the friend who probably gave him HIV is shown through his caring support as the other man lies dying of AIDS – and mirrors the care he receives in due course from Foster, to whom he probably transmitted the same virus; the lovers both have funerals at Easter (Brady, 2004) and are buried together in Kew Cemetery. Such is the level of connection which unites John and Juan in both life and death; such is Foster's skill that he can weave together such disparate threads of memory into a colourful tapestry of love and loss.

The book's original subtitle, *A Life Accomplished in the Era of AIDS*, was a refutation of Juan's deathbed exclamation of despair and defeat. This subtitle was deleted for the subsequent reissues, and may reflect the changing face of AIDS in Australia since Foster's book was first published.

The genre of Australian novel-length AIDS life narrative was a transitory and largely overlooked phenomenon; commencing with an autobiography by Eric Michaels (*Unbecoming: An AIDS Diary*, 1990) and ending with another by Robert Newey (*Lessons Learnt*, 2005); the arrival of new drug regimes then ended the conspicuousness of suffering and death. AIDS now inspires little interest within most Australians; they see it as affecting marginalised peoples who are geographically or emotionally distant from their own lives. This is another tragedy of the pandemic: we fail to recognise noble heroes and role models. As one character comments in Foster's book: 'I sense from your account ... that many people are increased in their humanity because of Juan's presence among them.'

John Foster's text is a story of humans and families: individuals, lovers, friends, biological versus adoptive families, religious and gay communities – and indeed the whole human family. In this mix, Juan is presented as both child and adult seeking his way in the world, while John Foster becomes both lover and mentor. The heartbreak of Juan's biological family as they lose him to refugee flight is counterbalanced with the pain faced by Juan's adopted Melbourne family as he fadeed away.

Take Me To Paris, Johnny has acquired extra layers of meaning since its initial publication. Juan originally escaped from Guantánamo in Cuba – a place which has taken on a new resonance around the world in more recent times as the location for other forms of cruelty – and his identity as a refugee also places his story within a more contemporary Australian context of discrimination and alienation. Most pointedly in recent times, the whole world has learnt what it means to endure under the spectre of pandemic. Foster could not have envisaged that his book would remain as relevant as tomorrow's headlines in the decades following his death.

John Foster shows his consummate skill as an author through his realism and compassion: love may not conquer all, but it makes everything bearable. His legacy is a work which echoes with the voice and essence of his departed friend, Juan Céspedes. In turn, readers can only wonder how many other Juans have been forgotten, with their stories left untold. Perhaps Juan's greatest accomplishment is that, in the pages of this memoir, he speaks on behalf of them all.

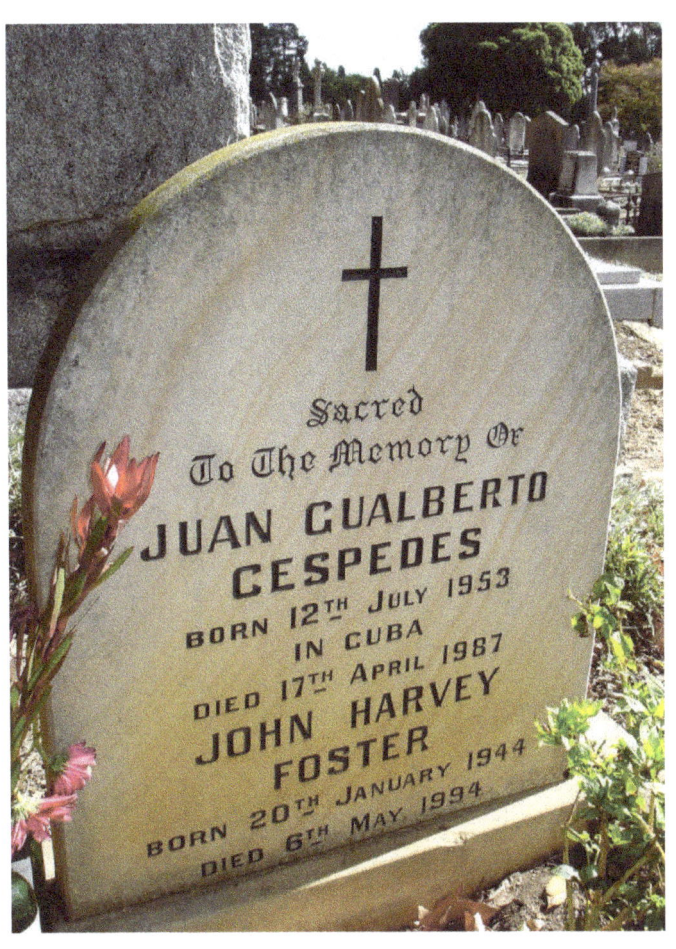

Gravesite of Juan Gualberto Cespedes and John Harvey Foster. Geoff Allshorn

FRIENDS ARE FOREVER

I belong to the generation that used to rely on a little address book to keep tabs on friends, family and possible dates for Saturday night. I recently skimmed through my old address book and was shocked to discover that most of the people within it are long dead.

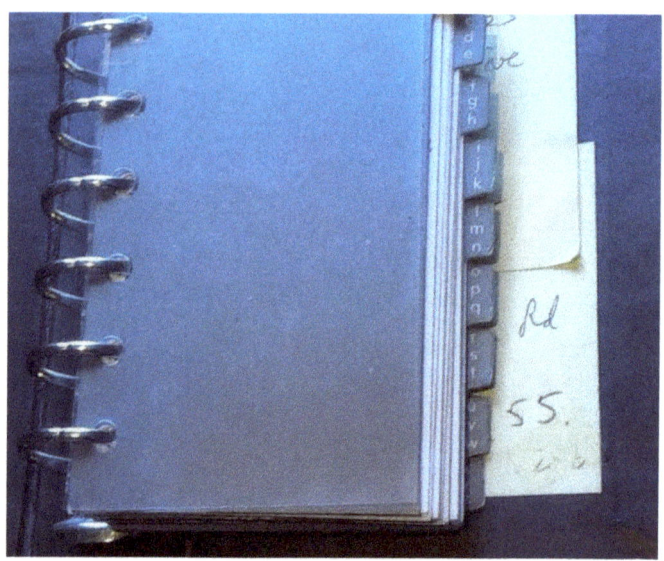

Address book – Geoff Allshorn

I remember visiting Tony in hospital. He had apparently recovered from his latest bout of illness, and was dressed, out of bed, and restlessly wandering the ward. He told me that he was looking forward to being discharged within days. We discussed getting a bunch of friends together to celebrate his discharge, and I left feeling positive that all was well. He died in hospital that night.

I visited Alex in hospital and the nurse led me into his single room with the loud, conversational comment that he was dying. That certainly put a damper on the visit! I suddenly became awkward and unsure of what to say. My training as an AIDS volunteer had not covered deathbed conversations, and I felt at a loss. He lay in bed looking miserable, and I stumbled through an awkward chat that was punctuated with long pauses. When I left, all too quickly, a wave of relief washed over me as I left the room, and he died shortly afterwards. I felt guilty for years that I had left him to die alone. Some years later, however, another friend told me that he had visited Alex later that same day and had held his hand while he died. My life experiences allowed me to learn and grow, and I have had many subsequent helpful and positive goodbye conversations as other loved friends have departed.

While the epidemic has been tragic and led to incalculable losses, it also introduced me to many, many people who enriched my life with friendship, wisdom, resilience and examples of courage and heroism..

I remember when a group of us went to see the movie, *Philadelphia* – except for John, who was unable to join us because he was sick – and we sat in a row and passed a box of tissues along the group as we wept during the AIDS scenes that symbolically depicted the lives of many of our friends. The next morning, we learnt that John had passed away while we were watching the movie. He would have liked the symbolism.

My elderly mother once remarked that I had been to more funerals than she had.

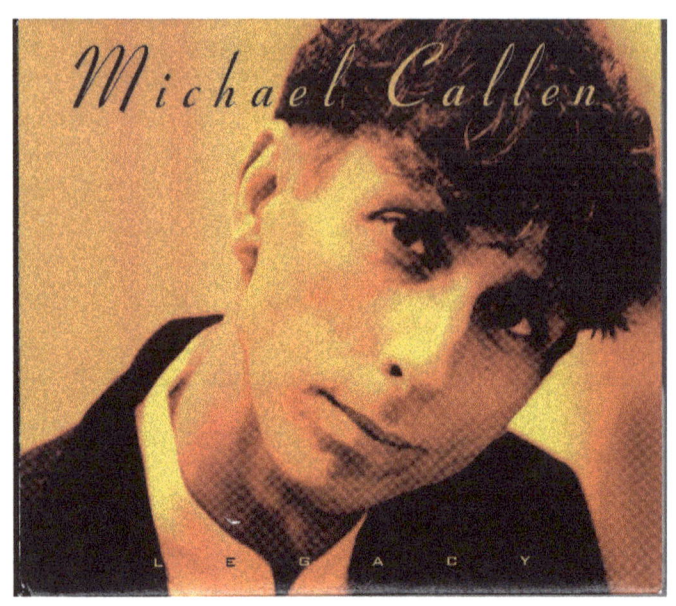

LOVE DON'T NEED A REASON

Michael Callen was a US singer and gay man who became an important AIDS activist during the terrible pandemic that swept the world in the 1980s and 1990s – and which continues to this day in many parts of the world. One of his legacy songs, *Love Don't Need A Reason*, was co-written by Australian-born singer Peter Allen (who also died of AIDS) and singer Marsha Malamet.

My personal introduction to Michael Callen took place through the US National March on Washington on 25 April 1993, not because I attended the event, but because I watched film clips from the March on the ABC News in Australia. I was visiting a lesbian friend who has since passed away, and we were captivated by Michael's song – a moment of beauty and peace during a stormy era when our civil rights were under attack and many of our friends were suffering and dying from a dreadful epidemic.

Michael Callen was a musician in The Flirtations, but his long list of activist achievements forms an impressive resume in itself. He rallied People With AIDS, formed support networks, led activist protests, wrote and edited activist books and literature, and appeared in a number of HIV/AIDS-related films (most famously 'Philadelphia') during an era of terrible stigma.

Although he came from a background where he had enjoyed a lifestyle of sexual freedom and 'promiscuity' within gay male communities, he later spoke against this behaviour in the era of AIDS, and expanded his activist work to support all who were affected by HIV/AIDS – women, children, minorities, haemophiliacs, and others.

He coined the term 'people with AIDS' (PWAs) to replace the early characterisations of PWAs as AIDS victims' and spoke of empowering them. He worked passionately for those with AIDS. He even helped to invent the then-revolutionary concept of safe sex. Impressive work for one individual – a musician by trade, an activist by calling.

I do not know if he considered himself a Humanist, but he was an atheist and he certainly undertook activist work that upheld Humanist principles, by working for the dignity of others and empowering the dispossessed. Although he testified to members of New York Congress in 1983 that, 'At age 28, I wake up every morning to face the very real possibility of my own death', the most recent book on his life and works notes that his atheism contained elements of 'hope and optimism' (Jones, 2020, 349), which I see as another Humanist trait.

Perhaps one of Michael's greatest gifts to the world was his strong hope. Author Sean Strub reports of Michael's 1990 book, *Surviving AIDS*, written at a time when HIV was largely seen as a death sentence. A gay cliché of dark humour during that same era was that *if life offers you lemons, make lemonaids*. This is what Callen did, not *denying* the world's problems but *defying* them; offering enlightenment to those facing darkness; offering a tomorrow for those whose today offers little. We can learn a lesson from him a generation later, whether facing cancer or COVID, poverty or prosperity, pride or prejudice. Australian AIDS historian Nick Cook recalls Michael Callen's 'show-stopping speech' at Australia's *Third National Conference on AIDS* in Hobart in August 1988, where he 'gave a rousing address about refusing to be ashamed of his infection' (Cook, 2020, 143). This encouraged, 'the first major coming out of people with HIV' in Australia, led by activists Chris Carter and Terry Giblett (Menadue, 2014, 20) – a virtual takeover of the conference by HIV-positive Australian activists gatecrashing the stage, coming out to the world –

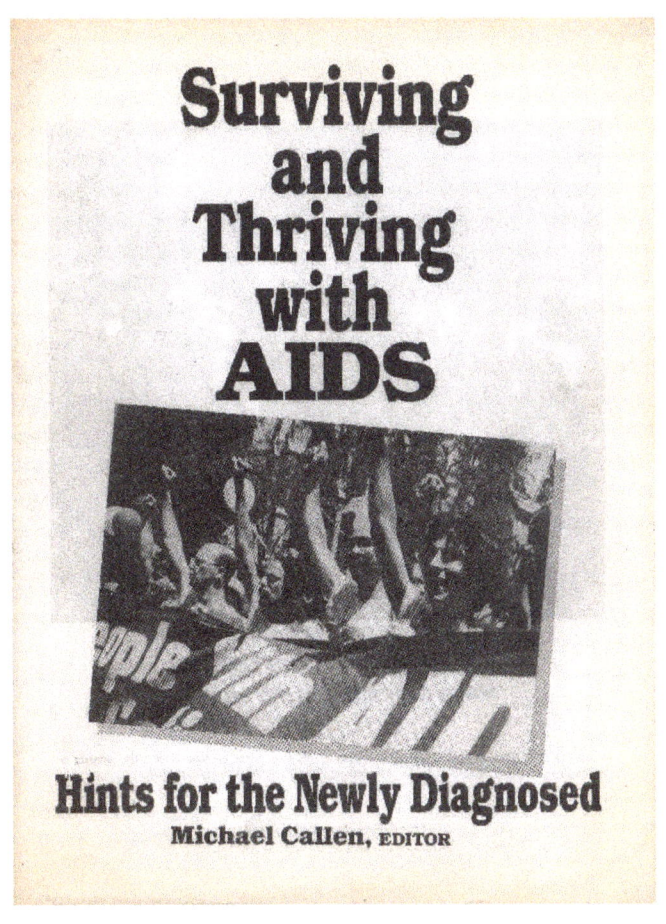

Surviving and Thriving with AIDS

Hints for the Newly Diagnosed

Michael Callen, EDITOR

and to each other – for the first time; amidst applause, cheers, tears, hugs and a standing ovation from the audience – in defiance of widespread stigma and discrimination across the nation (Cook, 2020, 144 – 150). In that event, Michael Callen changed Australia.

I am fortunate to own a copy of Michael's books, in one of which he has inscribed to its previous owner: '*Celebrate diversity and heal AIDS with love!*' Such words are surely worth remembering during this current pandemic and beyond.

Michael Callen died of AIDS at age 38 on 27 December 1993. We can only wonder what music, what activism, and what hope he might have offered the world during those fruitful years of life that he was denied. Maybe that is his last lesson to us: to grasp every day and every opportunity while we can. Because, as he says in his song: *love is all we have for now, what we don't have is time.*

Thank you, Michael.

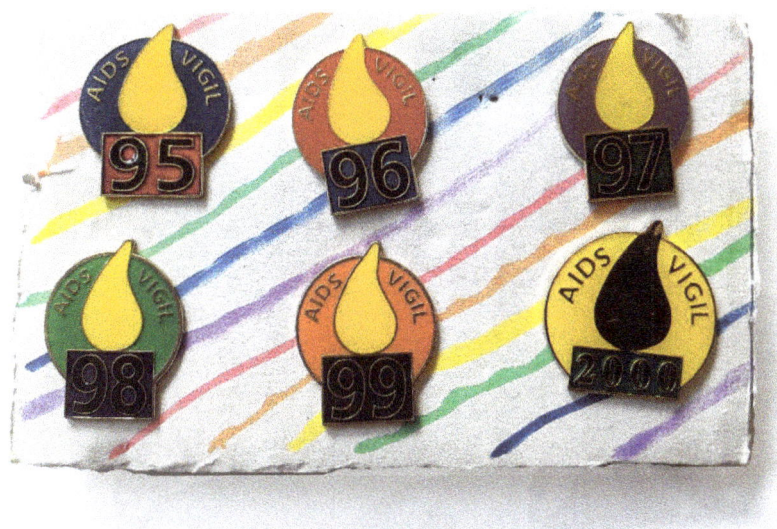

AIDS Vigil badges. Geoff Allshorn

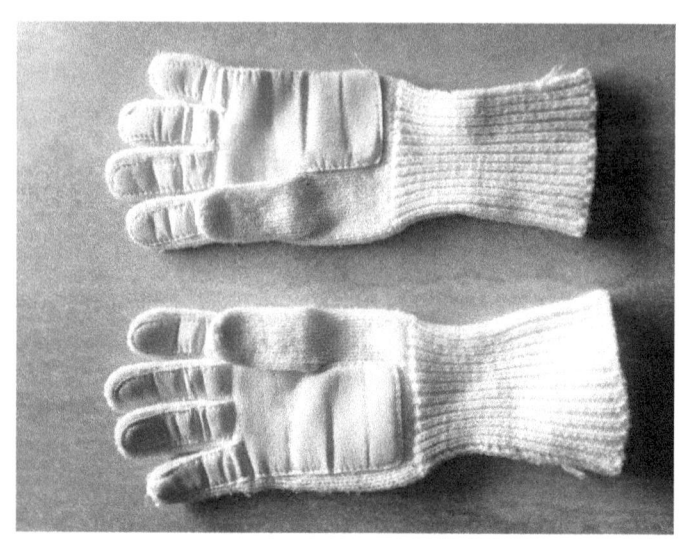

SEE IT AND UNDERSTAND

A pair of white gloves and a humble white scarf may not seem like particularly significant items from a wardrobe. But for me, they are reminders of possibly my most poignant time as an adult. I was in the midst of a war, and I met many noble warriors – many of whom died, and others who remain alive today after three decades.

The gloves and scarf are the only items of clothing I have left from my time with the AIDS Quilt. In those days, all Quilt monitors were required to wear white clothing from head to toe, in order to eliminate the possibility that any colourful clothing might otherwise somehow detract from the colours of the Quilt. I also seem to recall that in the USA, where the Quilt originated, white clothing was worn as a tribute to medical staff who offered palliative care to those who died with AIDS.

My gloves and scarf, and a small assortment of badges and other souvenirs, are my strongest personal reminders of those days.

Imagine a cemetery that was comprised of fabrics instead of tombstones. Instead of a mix of immovable concrete slabs and sombre grave plots, the memorial was a colourful, vibrant celebration of colour, individuality and celebration. Unlike static stone, it had the power for expansion, addition, community interaction and involvement; it was portable so could be taken to schools, community centers, hospitals, schools, parks or other public venues for display and pubic education.

Welcome to the AIDS Memorial Quilt – a community art project that allowed people to grieve, to publicly fight stigma, and to help educate the public by telling the stories of those lost to AIDS.

Individual Quilt panels were the size of a grave plot, sewed together into blocks of eight. Each panel was created by friends, lovers, partners, families, workmates, medical staff or activists in memory of someone who had been lost to AIDS.

Each panel reflected the personality of the person being memorialised, so each was different and unique: some displayed a sense of angry defiance – or sometimes a cheeky camp flair – aimed at honouring the person being remembered. Names and dates of birth and death, photos and personal items, rainbows, or photos of drag queens could be found amidst the teddy bears or leather straps.

In the early days of the epidemic, panels often lacked detail and might comprise only a first name. Early quilt panels were bare and sparse – but the personal identifying details expanded on later quilts, as panel makers became bolder and openly defiant in fighting the stigma.

In coming together to mourn and to grieve those who were lost to virus and to anonymity, their friends, families, loved ones and communities openly read aloud the names of the fallen and communed together in solidarity. As an atheist, I felt that the annual Quilt display was the closest thing to something being sacred that I had ever experienced.

I remember one panel that had been made by a family whom I got to know well in the months prior to the 1993 Quilt display. At that display, the panel lay on the floor of the Exhibition Buildings alongside the other new panels that year. Crowds were shuffling through the building to read, admire and ponder the many messages of love and grief …

One visiting young woman stopped as she saw this particular panel, with its photo of a cheeky young man and a loving tribute from his family. She quickly broke down and began to sob loudly. As a Quilt monitor, I moved over to her, offering her a tissue and a shoulder to cry on. I asked her if she had known this young man, and she looked momentarily startled. 'No,' she replied, pointing to the loving tribute, 'But it's just so sad …' and together, we hugged and wept.

A year or so later, I caught up with the parents of that young man, and told them about this young woman. They were profoundly moved that their son should, even in death, be able to teach others about love and compassion.

David Wootton wrote an article for a gay newspaper which revealed his feelings after his first ever visit to the Quilt in November 2000:

> *Although I felt sadness, I also felt immense pride – pride that so much love could be shown for people that [sic] faced more hate in their lives than anyone ever should … To me, the Quilt's message was not about sexuality, safe sex or even a disease. It was about the human spirit, the unbreakable bonds that people form, and memories that will never die.*

So why do I keep the gloves and scarf today, apart from simple utilitarian need? Why do I keep a small posey of flowers and herbs – once created by little old ladies and sold at LGBT festivals to raise money for the AIDS Quilt, but long since dried and bereft of smell or other practical purpose? Why do I keep a collection of badges that are little more than an historic relic of a past generation?

Because these things remind me of the power of volunteer work, of people collecting together to advance a common cause – of mums and dads and gay men and others working collaboratively to fight stigma and grief and discrimination. They remind me of the human spirit to which David Wootton alluded. And possibly most of all, I keep these items in order to honour the mandate of the Quilt Project: to keep the love alive.

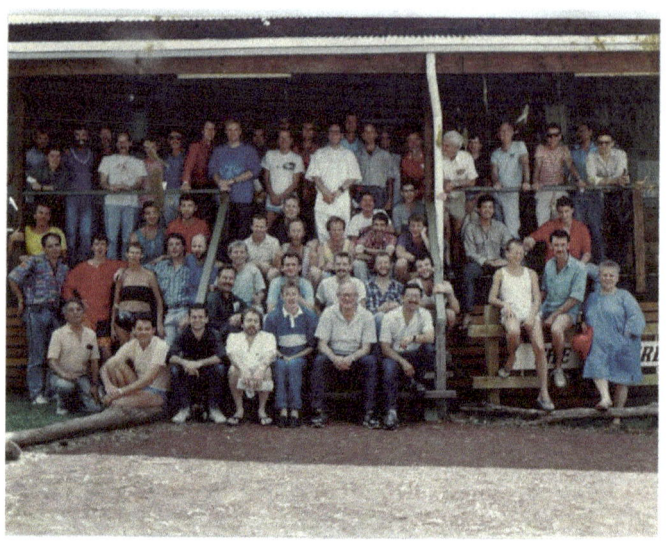

Support and other volunteers weekend away. Phil Carswell collection

HEROES OF THE EPIDEMIC

Watching the film Holding the Man *was a significant experience for me. I did not know Tim or John, but I did know some of their friends and associates, and I recognised some cameos in the film - people doing their bit to help incognito.*

It came nearly thirty years after Longtime Companion *became the first movie I ever watched that also portrayed LGBT people as normal, everyday people who were also confronted the abnormal situation of the same fatal virus.*

Holding the Man *gave me flashbacks to an earlier era, when a veritable army of volunteers came forward incognito to help those living (and dying) with AIDS. However, the covert nature of their voluntary work meant that we are unlikely to ever see their lives captured in biographical film.*

Imagine a virus that was significantly less infectious than COVID – not transmitted by normal social contact – and yet was stigmatised to the point where people often died alone and their families lied about their cause of death.

Imagine an epidemic where funerals and burials were often problematic because funeral homes often refused to take or treat the body – not because of transmission risk, but because of fear.

Imagine an epidemic where the greatest danger of transmission lay not in viral spread but in fear and prejudice and discrimination.

Now imagine a vast army of volunteers coming forward – secretly, respectfully – to offer love and palliative care to those who were dying.

I was a part of that army, and I observed loving kindness in action every day. Nurses, activists, housewives, mothers, gay men, families and others all worked together to care for the sick and dying.

People with AIDS were ferried from shopping expeditions to doctors' appointments, from haircuts to movie nights. Volunteers mowed their lawns, did their cooking and housework and laundry, and more. When necessary, they replaced bed sheets when night sweats overcame their clients; they toileted and cared for and hugged them, when most of society distanced themselves from those who were perceived to be unclean and diseased. They held hands with the dying, and then went home to their own unsuspecting families and households. I was surrounded by heroes. Gender considerations aside, Shakespeare spoke of them all: *He was a man. Take him for all in all, I shall not look upon his like again. – Hamlet, Act 1 Scene 2.*

The concept of 'Buddies' or 'AIDS Mates' or 'Care Teams' was first portrayed thirty years before 'Holding the Man' hit the silver screen. Independent US film maker Arthur J Bressan Jr. created 'Buddies' in 1985, two years before his own death from AIDS. The Aussie LGBT community took up the call from the start. This community rallying point became our way of life – and death – for some years, until modern medications reduced the mortality rate and turned HIV into a manageable condition.

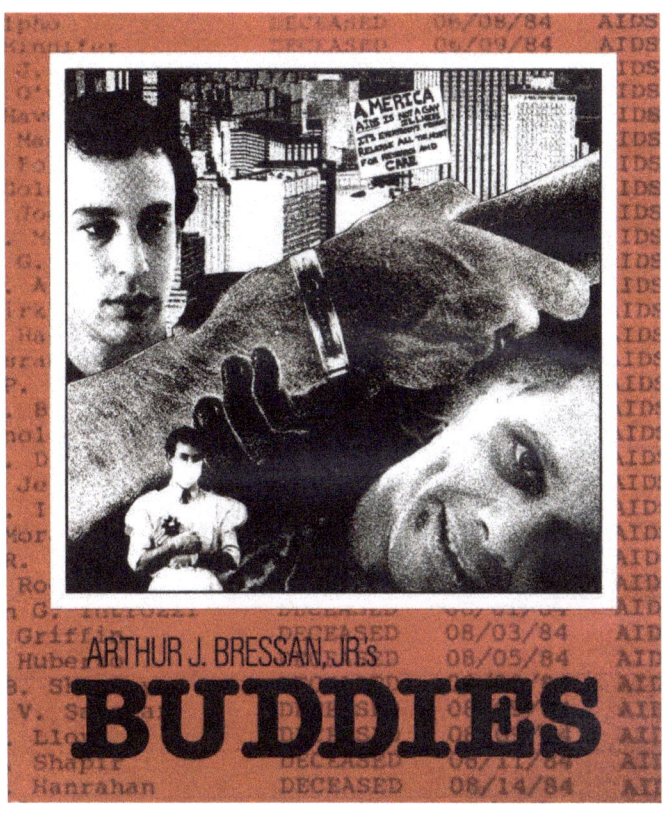

BLU-RAY Cover - *Buddies*

CHANGING THE WORLD

In 2017, marriage equality became Australian law. Millions of people rejoiced, and many activists breathed a huge sigh of relief. I wonder how many people paused to reflect on the memory of LGBT couples who, during the era of AIDS, were denied marriage equality, next of kin and inheritance rights, or familial and legal recognition? These earlier pioneers paved the way for a groundswell that later achieved marriage equality.

Public debate rages about the rights of religious schools to discriminate against LGBT teachers or students, the rights of religious employers to sack LGBT employees, or the welfare of LGBT people who might be compelled by family or churches to undergo 'gay conversion therapy'. Lest we forget the AIDS era, when LGBT teachers and students had no rights, when the idea of discrimination or reparative therapy was considered mainstream and normal, and when the welfare of LGBT people was popularly considered to comprise of their right to die of AIDS while being hidden away from polite society. Activists changed all these injustices, and modern generations often take LGBT equality for granted without understanding how their LGBT forebears had to literally fight for their lives.

Shoppers who buy a box of condoms from a supermarket shelf rarely recall the days when condoms were only available from behind the counter upon request at pharmacies – if the pharmacist did not have religious objections. While Dying with Dignity laws are enacted across Australia, nobody comments how this activism was spearheaded by those dying from AIDS in the 1990s. Needle exchange programs, community education programs that empower the communities that are most directly affected, harm minimisation programs, self help groups, and others, all owe their existence to the impact of AIDS activism.

To me, modern Australia is the ultimate example of being able to examine an historical artefact and see the layers of history underneath. Our lost friends and their work – they all live on.

When AIDS was announced to the world in 1981, it did not even have a name. It was just 'gay plague', or 'gay cancer' or 'gay pneumonia'. The Australian mass media largely ignored the problem, and the only way early LGBT activists could find or disseminate news and information, or to get help, was to do it themselves.

They changed their world and saved lives.

Community groups and organisations were founded, such as ACON, VAC, QuAC, ACSA and many others.

There was the Bobby Goldsmith Foundation, David Williams Fund, Positive Women, PLWHA groups, Straight Arrows, and many others designed to empower cohorts of people with particular HIV-related needs.

Volunteers flocked to Care Teams, the AIDS Quilt, Candlelight Vigils, AIDSline, and dozens of other groups that worked to educate, empower, and enact change.

There were Treatment Action groups, ACT-UP, and other activist groups designed to agitate for political, medical and social reform. And they got it.

The Australian model of self-empowerment became a model which has been upheld around the world as a leading model of community response to an existential threat. I am proud that I was able to become involved in even just one small part of this world-changing subculture. My memories live on, as does the world that activists created out of the disaster.

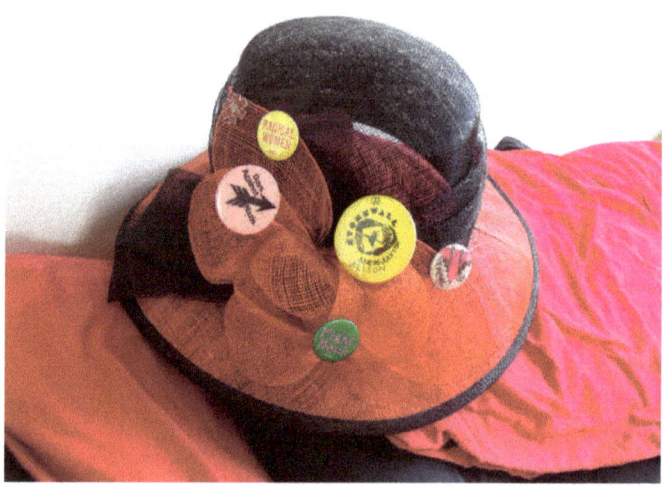

picture, Alison Thorne

The Victorian AIDS Council (VAC) has a quirky tradition of presenting people of all genders with a hat and a handbag when making them life members of the organisation. Alison was made a life member at the 2015 Annual General meeting along with a number of others who alongside her co-founded the Victorian AIDS Action Committee, the forerunner of VAC.

The badges, most from the early 80s, are from Alison's extensive collection. She has chosen them to symbolise her politics as a Marxist feminist. Her world view informed her intervention at public meeting held at the Royal Melbourne Dental Hospital on 16 June 1983 to share what was known about the emerging health crisis and discuss a community response to AIDS.

Alison, a member of both the Freedom Socialist Party and Radical Women, saw AIDS as presenting a political threat as much as a health threat to lesbians and gay men. As a passionate gay liberationist, she'd studied history and understood that the threat of a rightwing fuelled homophobic backlash was as real a menace to the community as the virus itself. Her call to band together, raise demands and organise a collective response found fertile ground.

Alison can be contacted at alison.thorne@ozemail.com.au. For more about the freedom socialist party see socialism.com. For more about Radical Women see https://www.radicalwomen.org

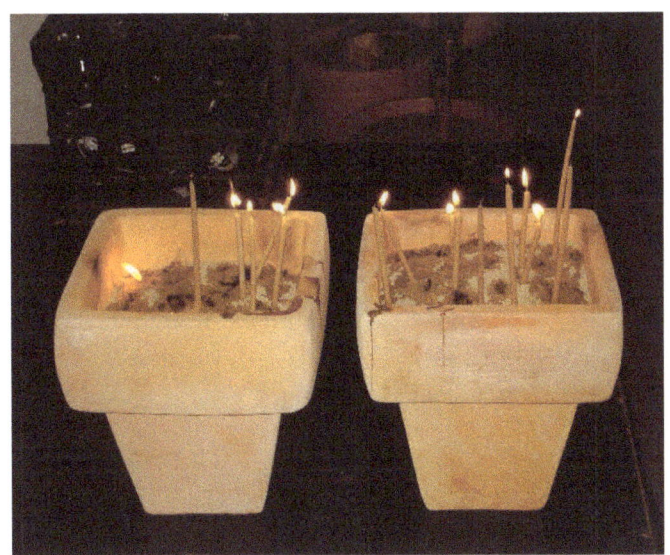

World AIDS Day Memorial 2005. Picture, Geoff Allshorn

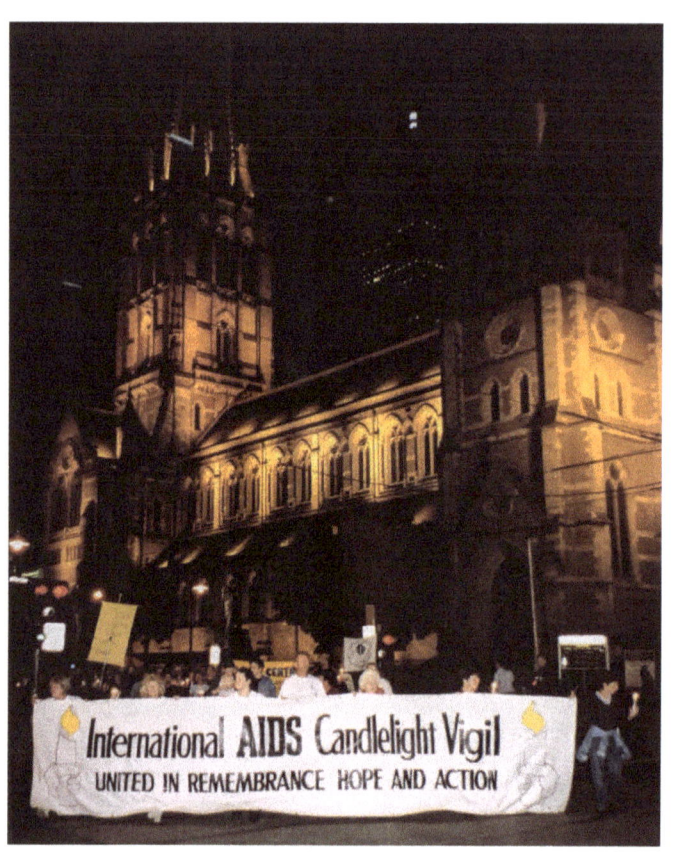

AIDS Candlelight Vigil. 1997. Geoff Allshorn

VIGIL

In 1997, five hundred people gathered in Melbourne, alongside the Polly Woodside (a famous sailing ship), then marched along Southbank and under Princes' Bridge towards the Sidney Myer Music Bowl in the Botanical Gardens.

The procession passed the Southbank shops and disappeared under Princes Bridge. As it reappeared on the other side of St. Kilda Road, it stretched along the footpath like a procession of fireflies in the twilight. I stood on Princes Bridge, above them, looking down at the marchers below, taking a photo of their candles in the gathering darkness ...

A gang of rough-looking teenagers approached me and asked me what was going on. I literally took a gulp before telling them about the AIDS Candlelight Vigil, and I silently steeled myself for a possible verbal or physical onslaught of homophobia or AIDS phobia. Instead, the nearest young man silently crossed himself as a sign of respect for the dead, and they deferentially moved on.

Even in their twilight years, the AIDS Candlelight Vigils lost none of their power to testify to lives, love and loss. Their legacy continues.

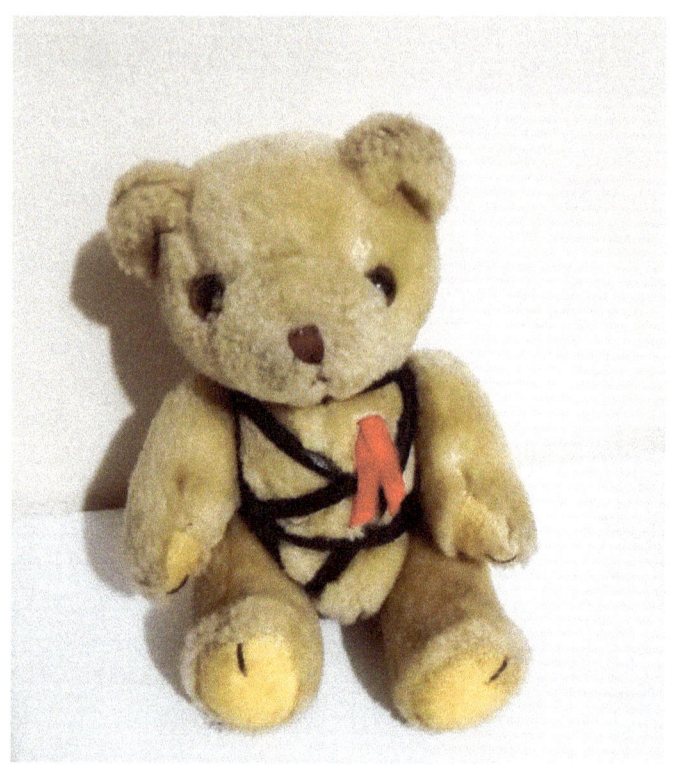

Cubbie. Geoff Allshorn

CUBBIE

Cubbie is a small, hand-sized cuddly bear. He wears leather and a red ribbon, just like his former owner, who had been a friend of mine,

I 'adopted' Cubbie after my friend died and his collection of bears was distributed to friends at his funeral.

Like Cubbie, my friend had also been a 'bear' and, like his cohort of leather community members, he had been hit early and hit hard by HIV/AIDS. Diagnosed in the early days of the epidemic, he was declared to have 'full blown' AIDS but managed to survive until the arrival of modern medications.

He was an activist in many LGBT/HIV/AIDS causes, and this is how I met him. He taught me a lot, and he features in many of my most significant activist memories.

He was a member of the AIDS Memorial Quilt Project and not only sewed a number of panels in memory of friends, but he also helped others mourn their losses when they came forward to add to the Quilt.

He was one of the activists who attended the only protest where I actually got to carry a placard SILENCE = DEATH in tribute to the ACT-UP protesters of past times.

He held the hand of a friend who died of AIDS, and comforted me when I later discovered that I had missed the chance to say goodbye to that same dying friend.

As a gay male atheist with AIDS, he visited churches and schools to help educate others about the affliction.

He died in 2017 from what I presume are complications related to his having lived with HIV/AIDS for nearly forty years.

In forty years from now, I wonder if survivors of COVID will be looking back at past times and past friends, mourning their losses and celebrating heroes from the epidemic.

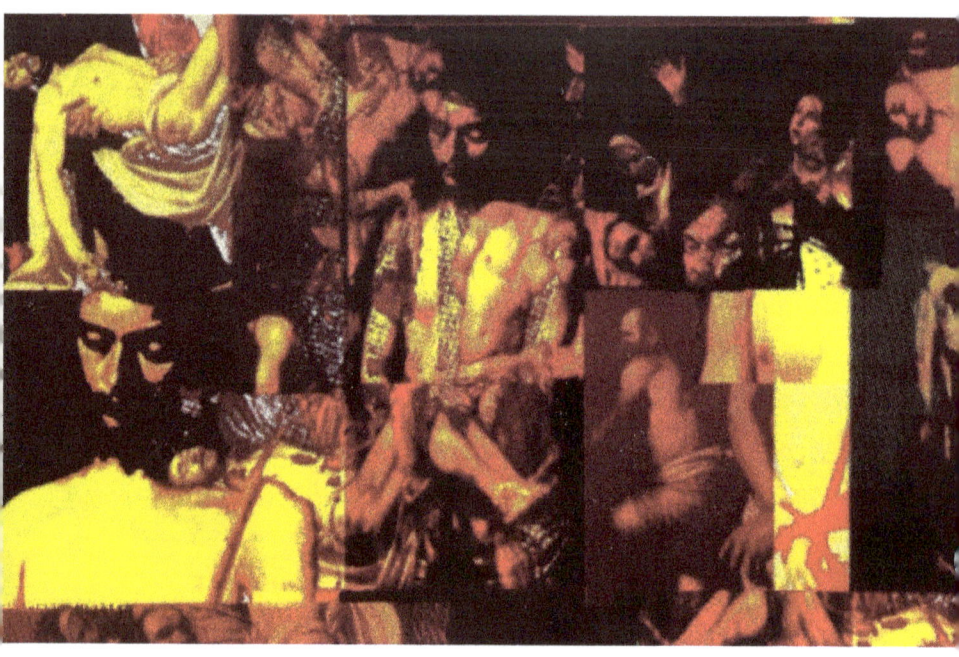

This is my body (detail). Marcus O'Donnell. Panel included in the 1994 National Gallery of Australia exhibition 'Don't Leave Me This Way: Art in the Age of AIDS'. Marcus O'Donnell

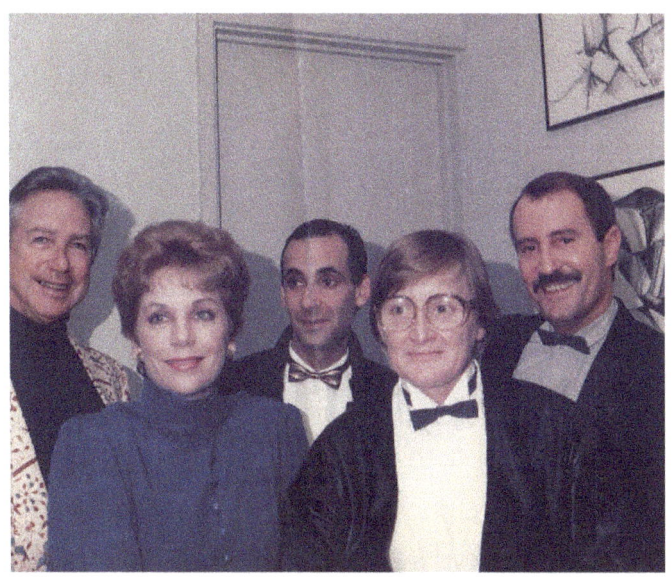

Fundraise at the Market Hotel, including Don Dunstan, Ita Buttrose and others. Undated. Phil Carswell.

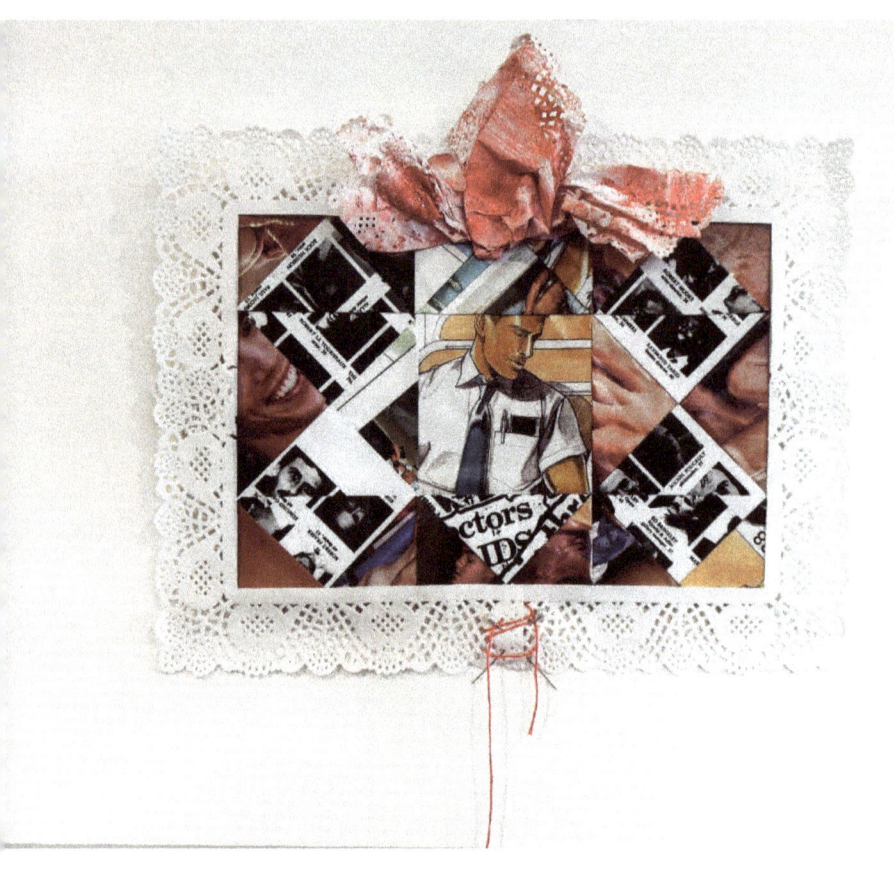

AIDS doily — Henry von Doussa

'I've been thinking a lot lately about the residue and ongoing trauma from HIV/AIDS in the gay community. HISTORICALLY, The QUILT is a mechanism for grieving, remembering and recovery. Making this artwork touched each area.' – Henry von Doussa

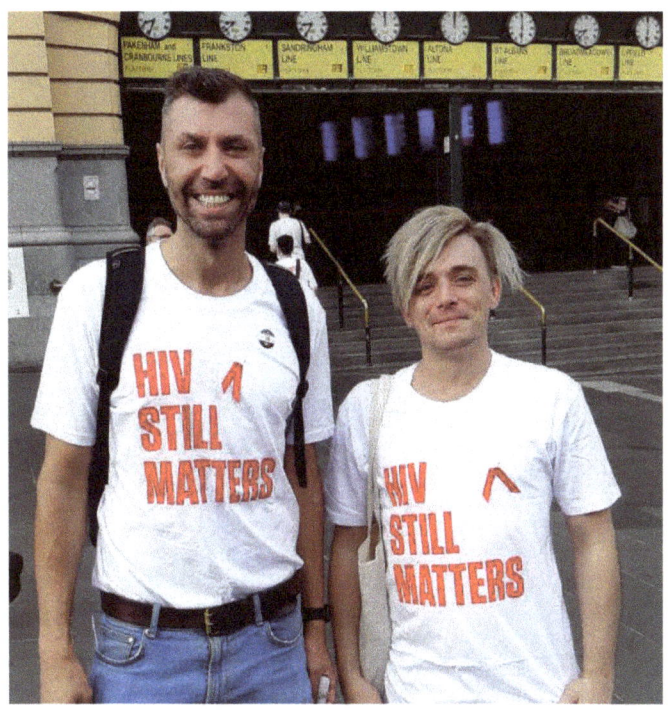

World AIDS Day, Melbourne . December 1, 2021. Community outreach.
Photo, Henry von Doussa.

This community activity organised by Thorne Harbour Health (formerly the
Victorian AIDS Council) - https://thorneharbour.org/

AFTERWORD

Around 2015 I was chatting to a gay man who was exactly twenty years my junior. He was complaining about how long it was taking for marriage equality to arrive.

'It sucks to be gay living in Australia today,' he moaned.

'It could be worse,' I replied without thinking. 'Like twenty years ago, when I was your age.'

He was puzzled, 'What was happening to gay people in Australia twenty years ago?' he asked.

I paused before replying. Where to start? Candlelight vigils, care teams, visiting dying friends in Fairfield Hospital.

On this World AIDS 2021, a year that marks the official arrival of AIDS in the world forty years ago, we pause and reflect that it is the time of a pandemic for another generation, and there are many lessons that we learned (or failed to learn from) an epidemic that still impacts the world.

In Australia and the western world we tend to think of AIDS as gone, forgotten, something in the past – like smallpox or polio. Nothing could be further from the truth. AIDS is still around. Though in many nations HIV is thoroughly manageable, due to medications, there are many places where HIV/AIDS is still a major concern.

I was recently contacted by an overseas LGBT refugee, living in poverty and deprivation. He confessed to me he was not feeling well, and when he sent me his photograph, my blood ran cold. I had a flashback to the 1980s and 1990s. No-one who was alive in those years will ever forget the photographs of thin, emaciated, skeletal young gay men who were then affected by what was then called 'full-blown AIDS'. I immediately knew what was wrong with this friend, and with his consent I was able to get medical intervention for him. He is now living quite happily and healthily in another location, away from where people might find out he has HIV.

On this day we reflect on the many heroes, and on the great courage that was shown in those early days and afterwards. Many of those activists became my personal heroes and mentors. Many – I'm privileged to say – are my friends and colleagues. What can we learn from them about human empathy, compassion, activism? During the early days of the epidemic we learned how to come together to agitate for political, social, and medical reform in the name of LGBTIQ and other human family. Do we do that today with COVID? Do we do it today for the LGBTIQ community? What do we need to learn from those people and those times a generation later?

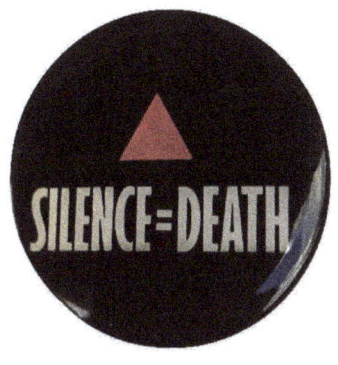

Forty years after the arrival of HIV/AIDS, there is still no vaccine. There are medications that make it a manageable lifelong condition. There are treatments that may hopefully create an AIDS-free world in years to come. And yet we still have so many things to learn. Why did the world get a vaccine for COVID within 12 months, and forty years on we're still waiting for a cure for HIV? What does this tell us about the world's priorities for oppressed, disempowered minorities? The old ACT-UP slogan, 'Silence = Death', asks us today: are we silent today about the plight of women around the world, indigenous people, LGBTIQ people? The Gay Liberation activists, and then the AIDS activists who succeeded them, would, I imagine, be among the first to passionately argue that our silence today still equals death.

Are we standing up for people in Africa, the Middle East, in Eastern Europe, South America, Asia, or anywhere where disempowerment and oppression still exists? Is the LGBT community in Australia too complacent? We have Marriage Equality. Is that the end of our human rights struggle? That's a question that should concern us all on World AIDS day, in 2021 and beyond. Where to from here?

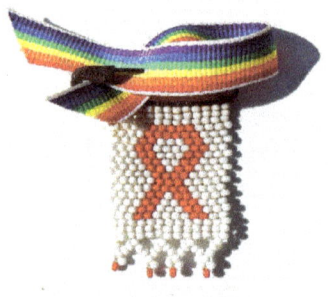

Lapel ribbon from South Africa. Collection pf Paul Cholewinski

SOMETHING HAS HAPPENED

An earlier version of this work appeared for the 40th anniversary of the *New York Times* article on the Humanist World blog at https://humanist-world.net/2021/07/03/something-has-happened/

REFERENCES

Carter, Helen, 1994. 'HIV Dates From '70s – Doctors,' in *The Herald Sun*, 7 March, 9.

Cochrane, Michelle, 2004. *When AIDS Began: San Francisco and the Making of an Epidemic*, Routledge.

Davies, Julie-Anne, 1993. 'Australia's First AIDS Death in 1981: Doctors,' in *The Sunday Age*, 7 November, 1.

Durvasula, Ramani, 2018. 'A history of HIV/AIDS in women: Shifting narrative and a structural call to arms', *Psychology and AIDS Exchange Newsletter*, American Psychological Association, March, at https://www.apa.org/pi/aids/resources/exchange/2018/03/history-women

Gerrard , John, et. al., 1994. 'Australia's First Case of AIDS?' in *The Medical Journal of Australia*, Vol. 160, 7 March, 247 – 250.

Grmek, Mirko D., 1990. *History of AIDS*, Princeton University Press.

Hooper, Edward, 1997. 'Sailors and star-bursts, and the arrival of HIV, *BMJ*, 315:1689–91.

- - - - - - - - - - -, 1999. *The River*, Allen Lane/Penguin Press.

Maj, Helle, 2020. 'Grethe Rask reddede liv på congolesisk missionshospital, indtil mødet med ukendt virus blev fatalt', *Kristeligt Dagblad*, 9 June, at https://www.kristeligt-dagblad.dk/udland/i-skovens-dybe-stille-ro. See also https://globalhealth.ku.dk/news/2020/after-hard-working-days-she-rested-by-the-beautiful-river-ebola/ for English translation by the University of Copenhagen.

Mankell, Henning, (translator Laurie Thompson), 2004. *I Die, But the Memory Lives On: The World AIDS Crisis and the Memory Book Project*, Harvill Press (Random House).

McKie, R., 1986. Panic: *The Story of AIDS*, Thorsens Publishing Group, UK.

Saxinger et al, 1985. 'Evidence for Exposure to HTLV-III in Uganda Before 1973', *Science*, American Association for the Advancement of Science, 1 March, Volume 227, pp. 1036-1038.

Serwadda, D, et al, 1985. 'Slim disease: a new disease in Uganda and its association with HTLV-III infection', *Lancet*, Volume 326, Issue 8460, 19 October: 849-52, at https://www.thelancet.com/journals/lancet/article/PIIS0140-6736(85)90122-9/fulltext

Shilts, Randy, *And The Band Played On*, Penguin Books.

Vangroenweghe, Daniel, 2001. 'The earliest cases of human immunodeficiency virus type 1 group M in Congo-Kinshasa, Rwanda and Burundi and the origin of acquired immune deficiency syndrome', *Philosophical transactions of the Royal Society of London, Series B: Biological Sciences*, 29 June; 356 (1410): 923-5, at https://www.ncbi.nlm.nih.gov/pmc/articles/PMC1088486/pdf/TB010923.pdf

Willis, Olivia, 2020. 'The man who died before his disease had a name', *Patient Zero*, ABC Radio National, 16 September, at https://www.abc.net.au/news/2020-09-16/mystery-death-rewrote-history-of-killer-disease-hiv-aids/12639410

Zhu, Tuofu, Korber, Bette, Nahmias, Andre. *et al.* 1998. 'An African HIV-1 sequence from 1959 and implications for the origin of the epidemic'. *Nature* 391, 5 February, 594–597, at https://www.nature.com/articles/35400

DEMARCATION

An earlier version of this work appeared for the 40th anniversary of the New York Times article on the Humanist World blog at https://humanist-world.net/2021/07/03/something-has-happened/

REFERENCES

Geoff Allshorn, 2011. *Heroes of the Epidemic: A Social History of HIV/AIDS in Melbourne during the 1980s*, unpublished Masters Preliminary thesis, La Trobe University.

Altman, Lawrence, 1981. 'Rare Cancer Seen in 41 Homosexuals', in *The New York Times*, 3 July, A20.

Author unknown, 1981. 'New pneumonia linked to gay lifestyle', in *Sydney Star*, Vol 2, No 25, 3 July, 2.

- - - - - - - - - - - , 2006. 'Interview with Cleve Jones', *Frontline: The Age of*

AIDS, PBS/WGBH Educational Foundation 3 May, accessed 21 September 2021, at https://www.pbs.org/wgbh/pages/frontline/aids/interviews/jones.html

Centers for Disease Control and Prevention, 1981. 'Pneumocystis Pneumonia — Los Angeles,' in *Morbidity and Mortality Weekly Report*. 5 June, 30 (21), 1-3.

------------------------------, 2001. 'Erratum' in 'HIV and AIDS --- United States, 1981—2000', *Morbidity and Mortality Weekly Report*, 1 June, 50 (21); 430-4, at https://www.cdc.gov/mmwr/preview/mmwrhtml/mm5047a10.htm

Foster, John, 1993. *Take Me To Paris, Johnny*, Minerva.

Garry, Robert F, *et al*. 1988. 'Documentation of an AIDS virus infection in the United States in 1968', *JAMA*, 14 October; 260 (14): 2085-7; abstract at https://jamanetwork.com/journals/jama/article-abstract/374422.

Maurer, Pattrice, 1992. 'Acting Up Against Junkie Pneumonia', *AGENDA*, Ann Arbor: Agenda Publications, 1, 4.

TV OR NOT TV

Anonymous, 'First Instinct' (episode review), *Packed to the Rafters* website, at http://au.tv.yahoo.com/packed-to-the-rafters/episodes/article/-/6124154/first-instinct/, accessed 6 April 2013, which refers to a character's HIV-status as 'the shocking truth'. Note that neither review actually states what 'the shocking truth' may be.

Peter Gawler (writer), 'Out Of Harm's Way', *Blue Heelers*, Episode 2.05 (050), telecast 21 March 21 1995, Channel 7, as reviewed by T. Zuk, *Blue Heelers Episode Guide: Series 2*, Australian Television Information Archive, at http://www.australiantelevision.net/bh/series2.html, accessed 9 March 2013.

Marieke Hardy (writer), 'First Instinct', *Packed to the Rafters*, Episode 2.14 (36), telecast 29 September 2009, Channel 7, reviewed by T. Zuk, *Packed to the Rafters Episode Guide: Series 2*, Australian Television Information Archive, at http://www.australiantelevision.net/packedtotherafters/series2b.html, accessed 9 March 2013

Peter Hawthorne, 'Positively Sesame Street', *Time* Magazine, 22 September 2002, at http://www.time.com/time/magazine/article/0,9171,353521,00.html #ixzz2GzIObgjb, accessed 4 January 2013.

Vicki Madden-Custo (writer), 'No Way Out', *Stingers*, Episode 3.06 (50), telecast 15 August 2000, Channel 9, as reviewed by T. Zuk, *Stingers Episode Guide: Series 3*, Australian Television Information Archive, at http://www.australiantelevision.net/stingers/series3.html, accessed 9 March 2013.

Kitty MacAlpine, 'A Country Practice: Dr. Terence Stephen Elliott', http://acountrypractice.com/Char/tselliott.html, accessed 7 November 2012.

Andrew Mercado, 'Super Aussie Soaps', Pluto Press, 2004, p. 170; James Davern, quoted in John Tulloch & Albert Moran, *A Country Practice: 'Quality Soap'*, Currency Press, 1986, pp. 260, 291, 292, 335, 346 – 350, 389.

Tony Morphett (writer), 'Return of the Hero', *The Flying Doctors*, Crawfords Productions, 1986.

Gerard J. Waggett, The Soap Opera Book of Lists,New York: HarperCollinsPublishers, 1996, p. 34.

Albert Moran, *Moran's Guide to Australian TV Series*, Australian Film and Television School/Allen & Unwin, 1993, p. 204

Harvey Shore, *GP: The Book of the ABC TV Series*, Sydney: ABC Enterprises, 1992, pp. 70, 71 &110.

TIME AND FRIENDSHIP

This work previously appeared on the 'Humanist World' blog at https://humanist-world.net/2021/08/08/time-and-friendship/

Dan McDonnell, 1988. 'A tragic test of friendship', in *The Sun*, Melbourne, 8 August.

FILM

Vito Russo, *The Celluloid Closet*, revised edition, New York: Harper & Row Publishers, 1987.

Roy Trakin, *Tom Hanks: Journey to Stardom*, London: Virgin Books, 1995, p. 174.

AND A CHILD SHALL LEAD

Uncle Paul Has AIDS by Phil Nott (author) and Sally Heinrich (illustrator),
    Nightcliff NT: Little Gem Publications, 1994.
Two Weeks with the Queen by Morris Gleitzman, Pan Macmillan, 1990
    (various reprints).
A Kid Called Troy by Vince Lovegrove, ABC Books, 1993.
Pink Balloons: The Story of A Young AIDS Sufferer by Beverley McGregor,
    Ashton Scholastic, 1995.

A TALE OF TWO CITIES

Original paper entitled, 'AIDS Response in San Francisco and Melbourne'
was presented at the 'Putting History In Its Place' Conference, La Trobe
University, 28 September 2012, and can be found here as part of the
conference program that was available on iTunes.

REFERENCES

Melbourne

Geoff Allshorn, 2011. *Heroes of the Epidemic: A Social History of
    HIV/AIDS in Melbourne during the 1980s*, unpublished Masters
    Preliminary thesis, La Trobe University.
W K Anderson, 2002. *Fever Hospital: A History of Fairfield Infectious Diseases
    Hospital*, Carlton South: Melbourne University Press.
Author unknown, n.d. 'Visitors to AIDS Conference' (undated note), Ian
    Goller Collection, Box 2 Folder 3, South Yarra: Australian Lesbian and
    Gay Archives.
John Ballard, 2003/2007. Untitled Review, in Neal Blewett, *AIDS in
    Australia: The Primitive Years: Reflections on Australia's policy response to the
    AIDS epidemic*, Sydney: Australian Policy Institute, University of
    Sydney, Commissioned Paper, 35 – 38.
Neal Blewett, 2003/2007. *AIDS in Australia: The Primitive Years*, Sydney:
    Australian Health Policy Institute, Commissioned Paper Series.
Phil Carswell, 1986. 'International AIDS Memorial' (Press Release by
    Victorian AIDS Council), 23 May.
Phil Carswell, 2009. Founding President's speech, VAC 25th anniversary

celebration, Fawkner Park, South Yarra, 5 April. Quote confirmed by private communication 25 September 2012.

Phil Carswell, 2009. Founding President's speech, VAC 25th anniversary celebration, Fawkner Park, South Yarra, 5 April. Quote confirmed by private communication 25 September 2012.

Adam Carr (ed.) 1986 (1990). *Meeting the Challenge: Papers of the First National Conference on AIDS*, Canberra: Australian Government Publishing Service, 1986; reissued Abbotsford: La Trobe University, 1990.

Adam Carr, 2011. 'When We Were Very Young: The Early Years of the HIV/AIDS Epidemic in Victoria', in Graham Willett, et al, eds, *Secret Histories of Queer Melbourne*, Parkville: Australian Lesbian and Gay Archives, pp. 149 – 152.

City of Melbourne, n.d. 'Melbourne in numbers', at http://www.melbourne.vic.gov.au/AboutMelbourne/Statistics/Pages/MelbourneSnapshot.aspx accessed 23 September 2012; dead link.

Timothy Conigrave, 1995. *Holding the Man*, Ringwood: McPhee Gribble.

Fairfield Hospital, 1994. *Annual Report and Financial Statement 1994*, Fairfield: Fairfield Hospital.

Fairfield Hospital, 1995. *Annual Report and Financial Statement 1995*, Fairfield: Fairfield Hospital.

John Foster, 1993. *Take Me To Paris, Johnny*, Port Melbourne: Minerva.

Ian Goller & Phil Carswell, 1985. International Conference on AIDS, Atlanta Georgia 14th – 17th April, Melbourne: Health Commission of Victoria, 1985, Ian Goller Collection, Box 2 Folder 2, South Yarra: Australian Lesbian and Gay Archives.

Lou McCallum, 2003/2007. Untitled Review, in Neal Blewett, AIDS in Australia: The Primitive Years, Sydney: Australian Health Policy Institute, Commissioned Paper Series, 2003/2007, pp. 32 – 38.

David Menadue, 2003. *Positive*, Crow's Nest: Allen and Unwin.

Prostitutes Collective of Victoria, n.d. *The Hussies Handbook: A Guide for Sex Workers and the Law*, St Kilda.

Prostitutes Collective of Victoria, n.d. *The Hussies Handbook: A Guide for Sex Workers and the Law*, St Kilda.

Allen Scroope & Phil Carswell, 1987. 'Report of Visit to San Francisco and Conference on Health Department Leadership and Community Response', Melbourne, Attachment 4: 'Shanti Project', Ian Goller Collection, Box 14 Folder 7, South Yarra: Australian Lesbian and Gay Archives.

VAAC News: Official Newsletter of the Victorian AIDS Action Committee, No. 1, October 1983, ALGA Collection.

VAAC News: Official Newsletter of the Victorian AIDS Action Committee, No. 2, March 1984, ALGA Collection.

San Francisco

Art Agnos, 1988. Quoted in *An Epidemic of Loss: AIDS in San Francisco's Gay Male Community 1988 – 1993*, report from conference of 30 October 1987, San Francisco AIDS Foundation, 25 March.

Author unknown, 1999. 'Estimated HIV Incidence, observed AIDS Diagnoses and projected AIDS Incidence' in National Centre in HIV Epidemiology and Clinical Research (ed.), *HIV/AIDS, Hepatitis C and Sexually Transmissible Infections in Australia: Annual Surveillance Report 1999*, Darlinghurst: National Centre in HIV Epidemiology and Clinical Research, Figure 2, p. 8.

Author unknown, n.d. San Francisco History Index, z Publishing.

Author unknown, Visitors to AIDS Conference, undated note, Ian Goller Collection, Box 2 Folder 3, South Yarra: Australian Lesbian and Gay Archives, accessed 20 September 2012.

Wyatt Buchanan, 2006. 'SAN FRANCISCO: Pride parade salute for an unlikely ally / Police officer who reached out in 1960s to be grand marshal', San Francisco Chronicle, 23 June.

Adam Carr, ed., *Meeting the Challenge: Papers of the First National Conference on AIDS*, Canberra: Australian Government Publishing Service, 1986; reissued Abbotsford: La Trobe University, 1990, pp. 196 – 203.

Focus: Bay Area Focused Growth, n.d. 'Population and Land Area', at http://www.bayareavision.org/bayarea/index.html, accessed 23 September 2012; dead link.

Matthew Kane, 'Screaming Queens: The Riot at Compton's Cafeteria', *Cineaste*, Volume 31 Number 4, Fall 2006, ProQuest Central, p. 104.

Susan Krohn, 1988. 'Agnos lobbies Washington AIDS – Reagan criticized for 'lack of leadership' on AIDS', United Press International, 26 March.

Gary Laderman, 2003. *Rest in Peace: A Cultural History of Death and the Funeral Home in Twentieth-Century America*, New York: Oxford University Press, pp. 140 – 144, 198 – 200.

Leon McKusick et al., 'AIDS and Sexual Behavior Reported by Gay Men in San Francisco', *American Journal of Public Health*, Volume 75 Number 5, May 1985, pp. 493 – 496.

Alex Pareene, 'Ronald Reagan cared more about UFOs than AIDS', Salon, 11 February.

John Phillips (writer) & Scott McKenzie (singer), 1967. *San Francisco (Be Sure To Wear Some Flowers In Your Hair)*, MCA Music Publishing.

Carol Pogash, 1992. *As Real As It Gets: The Life of a Hospital at the Center of the AIDS Epidemic*, New York: Birch Lane Press.

Everett M Rodgers, et al, 1995. 'Communication and Community in a City Under Siege: The AIDS Epidemic in San Francisco', *Communication Research*, Volume 22 Number 6, December, pp. 664 – 678.

Everett M Rodgers, et al, 1995. 'Communication and Community in a City Under Siege: The AIDS Epidemic in San Francisco', *Communication Research*, Volume 22 Number 6, December, pp. 664 – 678.

Office of the Mayor, n.d. 'Mayor Lee Announces U.S. Census Bureau Results for San Francisco Population', Office of the Mayor, City and County of San Francisco, at http://www.sfmayor.org/index.aspx?page=281; accessed 23 September 2012; dead link.

San Francisco History Index, n.d. 'A Timeline of San Francisco History: 1950 – Present', z Publishing.

E Stephen Searle, 1987. 'West Coast Lessons – AIDS in San Francisco', Health Education Journal, Volume 46 Number 3, pp. 130 – 133.

SFAF, 2010. 10 Moments that Changed History, San Francisco AIDS Foundation.

SFAF, 2012. The View from Here: Cleve Jones & Dr. Marcus Conant, San Francisco AIDS Foundation.

SFAF, 2021. 'SFAF History', San Francisco AIDS Foundation.

SFAF, 2021. 'SFAF History', San Francisco AIDS Foundation.

SFAF, n.d. (b). 'AIDS Walk San Francisco 1987', San Francisco AIDS Foundation.

Randy Shilts, 1987. *And the Band Played On: Politics, People and the AIDS Epidemic*, New York: St Martin's Press, 1987.

– – – 1992. 'Foreword', in Carol Pogash, *As Real As It Gets: The Life of a Hospital at the Center of the AIDS Epidemic*, New York: Birch Lane Press, pp. ix – xii.

Susan Stryker and Jim Van Buskirk, 1996. *Gay by the Bay: A History of Queer Culture in the San Francisco Bay Area*, Chronicle Books.

Lornet Turnbull, 2006. '12.9% in Seattle are gay or bisexual, second only to S.F., study says', *Seattle Times*, 16 November, at http://seattletimes.com/html/localnews/2003432940_gays16m.html, accessed 23 September 2012; dead link.

United Press, 1983. 'First Death from AIDS in Australia', San Francisco Chronicle, 11 July, ALGA collection.

US Census Bureau, n.d. 'Profile of General Population and Housing Characteristics: 2010 Demographic Profile Data', US Census Bureau: American Fact Finder, at http://factfinder2.census.gov/faces/tableservices/jsf/pages/productv iew.xhtml?src=bkmk; accessed 23 September 2012; dead link.

David Weisman, 2011. *We Were Here*, Peccadillo Pictures, 2011.

Other

Dennis Altman, 2001. *Global Sex*, Crows Nest: Allen & Unwin.

A. Leslie Banks, 1959. 'The Study of the Geography of Disease', *The Geographical Journal*, Vol 125, No. 2, June.

Lillian Faderman and Stuart Timmons, 2006. *Gay L.A.: A History of Sexual Outlaws, Power Politics, and Lipstick Lesbians*, New York : Basic Books, 1 & 2.

Laurie Garrett, 1995. *The Coming Plague*, New York: Penguin Books.

Colin Gordon (ed.), 1980. *Michel Foucault: Power/Knowledge, Selected Interviews and Other Writings*, New York: Pantheon Books.

Colin Gordon (ed.), 1980. *Michel Foucault: Power/Knowledge, Selected Interviews and Other Writings*, New York: Pantheon Books.

Lynda Johnston and Robyn Longhurst, *Space, Place and Sex: Geographies of Sexuality*, Maryland: Rowman and Littlefield Publishers Inc, 2010.

Jacques M May, 1953. 'The Geography of Disease', *Scientific American*, Volume 188, Issue 2, 02/1953.

Simon Naylor, 2008. 'Historical Geography: Geographies and Historiographies', *Progress in Human Geography*, Volume 32, Issue 2, 265 – 274.

Dr John Snow, 1855. 'Dr. Snow's Report,' in Report on the Cholera Outbreak in the Parish of St. James, Westminster, during the Autumn of 1854, in Peter Vinten-Johansen, *The John Snow Archive and Research Companion*, accessed 20 September 2012 and 5 May 2021.

Previously published at 'Humanist World' blog at https://humanist-world.net/2021/05/18/a-tale-of-two-cities/

MAKING MUSIC

Alex Harding, Fly Away (see https://www.theatrepeople.com.au/only-heaven-knows/)

BECOMING

Stuart Cunningham, 'Michaels, Eric Philip (1948–1988)', Australian Dictionary of Biography, National Centre of Biography, Australian National University, published first in hardcopy 2012, accessed online 14 November 2021.

Paul Foss, 1990. 'Foreword' in Eric Michaels, 1990b.

John Hobson, n.d (a). *Queers of the Desert* AIDS Quilts (1990).

John Hobson, n.d (b). *Queers of the Desert:* Eric Michaels.

Eric Michaels, 1987. *For A Cultural Future: Francis Jupurrurla Makes TV at Yuendumu*, Melbourne: Artspace.

Eric Michaels, 1990a. 'A model of teleported texts (with reference to Aboriginal television)', in Tom O'Regan (ed.), 1990, *Communication and Tradition:* Essays after Eric Michaels, Continuum: The Australian Journal of Media & Culture, Vol. 3, No. 2.

Eric Michaels, 1990b. *Unbecoming: An AIDS Diary*, Rose Bay: EMPress.

Eric Michaels, 1994.'Aboriginal Content: Who's Got It, Who Needs It?', *Bad Aboriginal Art: Tradition, Media, and Technological Horizons*, Minneapolis: University of Minnesota Press, 21 – 48.

Tom McLean, 1989. *If I Should Die: Living With AIDS*, Glenfield: Benton Ross Publishers.

Tom O'Regan (ed.), 1990. 'Preface', *Communication and Tradition:* Essays after Eric Michaels, Continuum: The Australian Journal of Media & Culture, Vol. 3, No. 2.

PA, 1989. 'Author dies of A.I.D.S.', *The Christchurch Press*, 27 March.

Article previously published on humanist blog etc etc at https://humanist-world.net/2021/12/01/7746/

DO YOU REMEMBER?

This article was previously published on 'Humanist World' blog at
https://humanist-world.net/2021/04/17/do-you-remember-the-era-of-aids/

REFERENCES

Mark Baker, 1994. 'Gentle Critic of the Hills Hoist Culture', in Michael
 Visontay (editor), 'Time and Tide' (obituaries), *The Australian*, 18 May
 1994, p. 16.
Jim Brady, 1994. 'Eulogy', in Baker, Mark, editor (1997), *History on the Edge:
 Essays in Memory of John Foster 1944-1994*, University of Melbourne
 History Department.
Peter Craven, 1994. 'A Rare Thing', in *Voices*, Vol. IV Number 2, Winter, pp.
 118 – 122; an excerpted version of this essay was reprinted as the
 Foreword to the 2003 reissue of John Foster's book.
Robert Dessaix, 1994. 'The Dark Rose', in *Meanjin #1*.
Stephen Dow, 2003. 'AIDS, Fragile Love and Dying', in *The Age*, 28
 September, *Agenda* section, p. 10.
John Foster (editor), 1986. *Community of Fate: Memoirs of German Jews in
 Melbourne*, Allen & Unwin.
John Foster, 1993. *Take Me To Paris, Johnny*, Minerva.
John Foster (reissue), 2003. *Take Me To Paris, Johnny*, Black Inc. (includes
 Foreword by Peter Craven and Afterword by John Rickard).
John Foster (reissue), 2016. *Take Me To Paris, Johnny*, Text Publishing
 Company. (includes Foreword by Peter Craven and Afterword by John
 Rickard).
Robin Grove, 1994/1995. 'A Memory's Shape', in *Island* No 60/61,
 Spring/Summer, pp. 68-71. (Note: this article contains a beautiful
 photograph of Juan which is not available in any of the other literature).
John Hanrahan, 2003. 'Loving and Dying', in *Australian Book Review*,
 November.
Tom Mclean, 1989. *If I Should Die: Living With AIDS*, Benton Ross
 Publishers, p. 56.
John Rickard, 2003. 'Afterword', in John Foster, 2003, as above.
Ian Robertson, 1994. 'Obituary: John Foster', in *The Age*, 14 May, 'Extra' p. 8.
Winston Wilde, 2008. *Legacies of Love: A Heritage of Queer Bonding*, Haworth
 Press.
Stephen J Williams, 1994. 'The Personal Will Be History, One Day',

in *Overland* No. 136, Spring, pp. 84 & 85.

Hugh Young, 2002?a. 'HIV/AIDS in New Zealand', in *Queer History New Zealand: Gay, Lesbian, Bisexual and Transgender New Zealand History*, Queer History NZ.

— — — — — — 2002?b. 'A Chronology of Homosexuality in New Zealand: Part 5 – From Law Reform to the Present', in *Queer History New Zealand: Gay, Lesbian, Bisexual and Transgender New Zealand History:* Part 5, Queer History NZ.

LOVE DON'T NEED A REASON

An earlier version of this article appears on the Humanist World blog at https://humanist-world.net/2021/04/24/love-dont-need-a-reason/

REFERENCES

Berkowitz, Richard & Callen, Michael, with editorial assistance by Dworkin, Richard (1983). *How to Have Sex in an Epidemic: One Approach*, New York: News From the Front Publications, May.

Callen, Michael, ed. (1987). *Surviving and Thriving with AIDS*, New York: People With AIDS Coalition Inc.

Callen, Michael, ed. (1988). *Surviving and Thriving with AIDS Volume Two: Collected Wisdom*, New York: People With AIDS Coalition Inc., August.

Callen, Michael (1990). *Surviving AIDS*, New York: HarperCollins.

Cook, Nick (2020). *Fighting For Our Lives: The history of a community response to AIDS*, Sydney: NewSouth Publishing/University of New South Wales Press Ltd.

Jones, Matthew T (2020). *Love Don't Need a Reason: The Life & Music of Michael Callen*, punctum books, 11 May.

Menadue, David (2014). 'Stigmatised but largely invisible', in John Rule, ed., *Through our eyes: Thirty Years of people living with HIV responding to the HIV and AIDS epidemics in Australia*, Newtown: NAPWHA, July, 18 – 21.

Strub, Sean (2014). *Body Counts: A Memoir of Politics, Sex, AIDS, and Survival*, New York: Scribner.

SEE IT AND UNDERSTAND

(David Wootton, 'Rites of passage', *Melbourne Star Observer*, 17 November 2000, p. 4)